Contents

Annexes

List of figures

List of tables

Summary of pages

This document comprises a front cover, an inside front cover, pages i to iv, pages 1 to 74, an inside back cover and a back cover.

Foreword

Publishing information

This Published Document was published by BSI and came into effect on 31 August 2006. It was prepared by Technical Committee MS/2, *Project management*. A list of organizations represented on this committee can be obtained on request to its secretary.

Relationship with other publications

BS 6079 is published in four parts:

- Part 1: *Guide to project management*;

- Part 2: *Vocabulary*;

- Part 3: *Guide to the management of business related project risk*;

- Part 4: *Guide to project management in the construction industry*.

Parts 1 to 3 are generic to all industry sectors. Part 4 is an interpretation of BS 6079-1 for the construction industry.

This Published Document should be read in conjunction with the latest edition of BS 6079-1.

Use of this document

As a guide, this Published Document takes the form of guidance and recommendations. It should not be quoted as if it were a specification and particular care should be taken to ensure that claims of compliance are not misleading.

Any user claiming compliance with this Published Document is expected to be able to justify any course of action that deviates from its recommendations.

Presentational conventions

The provisions in this Published Document are presented in roman (i.e. upright) type. Its recommendations are expressed in sentences in which the principal auxiliary verb is "should".

Commentary, explanation and general informative material is presented in smaller italic type, and does not constitute a normative element.

Contractual and legal considerations

This publication does not purport to include all the necessary provisions of a contract. Users are responsible for its correct application.

Compliance with a Published Document cannot confer immunity from legal obligations.

Attention is drawn to the Construction (Design and Management) Regulations 1994 and subsequent amendments [1].

Introduction

This part of BS 6079 is issued as a Published Document to allow for further comment before publication of the guide as a British Standard in 2007. It provides an industry-specific interpretation of the generic guidance provided by BS 6079-1.

The guide sets out the principles and processes of project management as they apply to construction projects irrespective of scope, size or organization of the project. The processes, and the issues highlighted, are relevant to all projects and to all types of contractual arrangement; although the extent to which each is relevant in particular circumstances will be a matter for considered judgement, dependent on the scale, complexity and nature of the project in question.

It is applicable to projects involving the construction of buildings, civil engineering works (roads, railways, airports, ports and harbours, sea and river works, etc.), mechanical and electrical works, infrastructure works, and to energy and process plants (power plants, refineries, chemical plants, etc.). It is also applicable to projects involving repair and maintenance of these works.

Its advice is designed to be equally applicable to a project manager working for a specialist subcontractor managing an element of the construction, or the ultimate client's project manager with overall responsibility for the client's entire project.

Figure 1 sets out the structure of the guide. It has been designed to provide a clear, logical approach to the process of producing a project management plan for a project, whether that be the client's entire project or a subcontractor's project represented by the subcontractor's works. This document formally sets down how a project should be managed. Such a plan is a pre-requisite to good project management, embodying all the processes necessary to achieve a successful project.

Figure 1   **Structure of PD 6079-4**

Document section	Content
Scope	**Clause 1** Purpose and aims of the guide
Normative references	**Clauses 2 and 3** Definitions
Terms and definitions	
Project management in construction	**Clause 4** Characteristics of the construction industry, and the role of project management
Project management plan (PMP)	**Clause 5** Introducing the project management plan – the document that draws together the processes that are used to manage the project
Project scope definition	**Clause 6** Establishing a business case and the brief from the client for the project
Project organization structures	**Clause 7** Designing the project organization
Life cycle	**Clause 8** Understanding the project lifecycle introducing review, control, and authorization points
Product delivery / Project management processes / Regulatory processes	**Clauses 9, 10 and 11** The product delivery process – the core process of design and construction and The regulatory and enabling processes – the processes that run concurrently with the product delivery process, ensuring compliance with statute and best practice Application of the project management processes to both
Project management processes	**Clause 11** The core project management processes used to manage and control a project

1 Scope

This Published Document is a guide to project management in the construction industry in its broadest sense. It deals with the construction process from inception through to handover of the completed facility to the owner, occupier or operator. It is also applicable to projects involving the maintenance, repair, refurbishment, decommissioning and demolition of existing facilities. Its guidance is relevant to both domestic and international projects and to all project participants including clients, professional consultants and designers, and contracting organizations including managing contractors, main contractors, specialist works contractors, subcontractors and suppliers.

The guidance is equally applicable to the management of the many supporting projects or subprojects, commonly termed contracts and subcontracts, undertaken by technical specialists, contractors, subcontractors or suppliers, and to the management of the ultimate client's project, i.e. the project promoted by the industry's customer.

2 Normative references

The following referenced documents are indispensable for the application of this document. For dated references, only the edition cited applies. For undated references, the latest edition of the referenced document (including any amendments) applies.

BS 6079-1:2002, *Project management – Part 1: Guide to project management*

BS 6079-2, *Project management – Part 2: Vocabulary*

BS 6079-3, *Project management – Guide to the management of business related project risk*

BS 8800, *Occupational health and safety management systems – Guide*

BS EN ISO 14001, *Environmental management systems – Requirements with guidance for use*

BS ISO 10006, *Quality management systems – Guidelines for quality management in projects*

OHSAS 18001, *Occupational health and safety management systems – Specification*

3 Terms and definitions

For the purposes of this Published Document, the terms and definitions given in BS 6079-1, BS 6079-2 (except where amended below), BS ISO 10006 and the following apply.

3.1 client

person or organization that commissions a project

3.2 change management

assessing the impact of proposed changes on the scope or timing of a project, authorizing and implementing the change, monitoring and recording it, irrespective of who generated the change

NOTE   *The objective is to make all parties fully aware of the cost, time and quality implications of implementing such changes. Change management is also referred to as variations management, compensation events or change control.*

3.3 configuration management

process of managing the configuration (i.e. product design and specification) of a project's product(s)

3.4 construction management

contractual agreement where the client employs a professional management team to coordinate works contractors directly employed by the client

3.5 contract administration

task of carrying out the procedural and administrative functions that govern the relationship between client and supplier and that are prescribed in a construction contract

3.6 contract administrator

person responsible for the administration of a contract

3.7 control point

point in time or in a project schedule at which to revalidate the objectives of the project, and to reconfirm key parameters such as scope, cost and schedule

NOTE   *Usually at the end of key phases or stages of the project lifecycle. Also referred to as gateways, authorization points and check points.*

3.8 framework agreement

agreement between a client and supplier, for the supplier to do a particular type of work for the client for a fixed period of time

NOTE 1   *The framework agreement will last for a stated period of time, subject to successful periodic evaluations.*

NOTE 2   *There can also be framework relationships between suppliers, e.g. between contractor and subcontractors.*

3.9 operator

person or organization to whom a product is handed on completion

NOTE   *The operator might sometimes be the end user.*

3.10 partnering

management approach used by two or more organizations to achieve specific business objectives by maximizing the effectiveness of each other's resources and minimizing conflicts

NOTE 1   Other terms often used in the construction industry are alliancing, frameworks, extended arm.

NOTE 2   Partnering can be project-specific or for a series, or programme, of projects.

3.11 product

project deliverable

EXAMPLE   In the context of the overall project, this could be a building, a road, a power station, etc. In the case of a subproject it could be a planning application, or an element of the works e.g. the curtain walling.

3.12 project

overall system and processes that will deliver a product
[amended from BS 6079-2:2000, definition **2.116**]

3.13 project control

processes used to control scope, quality, cost or time on a project or process

3.14 project process

set of linked activities that take place in accordance with certain rules and convert inputs to outputs

3.15 project schedule

time plan for a project or process
[amended from BS 6079-2:2000, definition **2.134**]

NOTE   On a construction project this is usually referred to as a "project programme". The construction industry tends to refer to programmes rather than schedules. Indeed the term "schedule" tends to mean a schedule of items in tabular form, e.g. door schedule, ironmongery schedule, etc.

3.16 project team

team of individuals and organizations responsible to the project manager for undertaking a project
[amended from BS 6079-2:2000, definition **2.136**]

3.17 stakeholder

person or group of people who have a vested interest in the delivery and outcome of a project
[amended from BS 6079-2:2000, definition **2.167**]

NOTE   This interest could be in either a positive or a negative outcome.

3.18 subproject

fully self-contained project, but a project that is itself only a part of the larger project being undertaken on behalf of the ultimate client

NOTE   A works contract, for example, is a subproject. The term is used in this Published Document as a convenient way to differentiate a subproject from the main client project, but a subproject will have all, or most of, the attributes of the client's project, and the guidance provided herein is fully applicable.

3.19 supplier

individual or organization that is a provider of services or products

4 Project management in the construction industry

4.1 General

This clause looks at the make-up of the construction industry and its characteristics, before explaining the role of project management and the project manager.

4.2 The construction industry and construction industry projects

4.2.1 Characteristics on the construction industry

An appreciation of the characteristics of the construction industry is valuable before considering the application of project management to projects. The industry services an extremely broad client base and projects are diverse in their nature, size, scope and location. Table 1 sets out some of the characteristics of the industry.

Table 1   **Characteristics of the construction industry**

Characteristic	Examples
Diversity of clients	Government, public sector body, company, partnership, private individual
Diversity of project type	Function, scope, size, complexity, value, location Building, civil engineering, mechanical and electrical, IT, communications, process plant, multi-disciplinary New build, refurbishment, repair, maintenance, renewal
Diversity of project objectives	Scope, level of quality, criticality of time, criticality of cost and cash flow
Site location factors	Operational "live" environments, greenfield, brownfield, marine, underground, local, national, international, neighbours, climate, custom and practice, e.g. taxes, etc.
Diversity of project participants	Clients, consultants, contractors, subcontractors, suppliers, occupiers and operators, neighbours, third-party stakeholders, statutory and regulatory bodies, funders (Many participants involved at different stages of the process)
Diversity of disciplines involved	Clients (any industry sector), specialist consultants, designers, lawyers, contractors, fabricators, suppliers, labourers, etc.
Regulatory requirements	Health and safety, sustainability, environmental, town and country planning, building control, land and property, statute
Industry custom and practice	Established institutions, established roles and responsibilities, established contracting arrangements, established procurement strategies, established conditions of contract, law, etc.
Technology	Very basic to highly complex, traditional to state of the art
People	Highly qualified professionals, skilled trades people, skilled labour, general labour (low skills) Variable quality, variable experience, itinerant work force
Organizational structures	Teams come together for a finite period of time to deliver a project or series of projects Numerous separate organizations – designers, consultants, contractors, suppliers, third parties, regulatory bodies, etc.
Management	Variable quality, experience, skills, expertise Focused around industry custom and practice and the traditional conditions of contract
Quality	Variable – people, products, systems and processes, design standards
Work locations	Office, design office, fabrication shop, site

All of these factors can have the potential to influence and affect a project, and need to be considered when developing a management system for a project.

Successful project management requires the management of quality, cost and time, underpinned by safety. This often necessitates compromise with priority given to two of the three constraints. However safety cannot be compromised in any circumstances on construction projects. Figure 2 shows the constraints.

Figure 2   **The project management triangle**

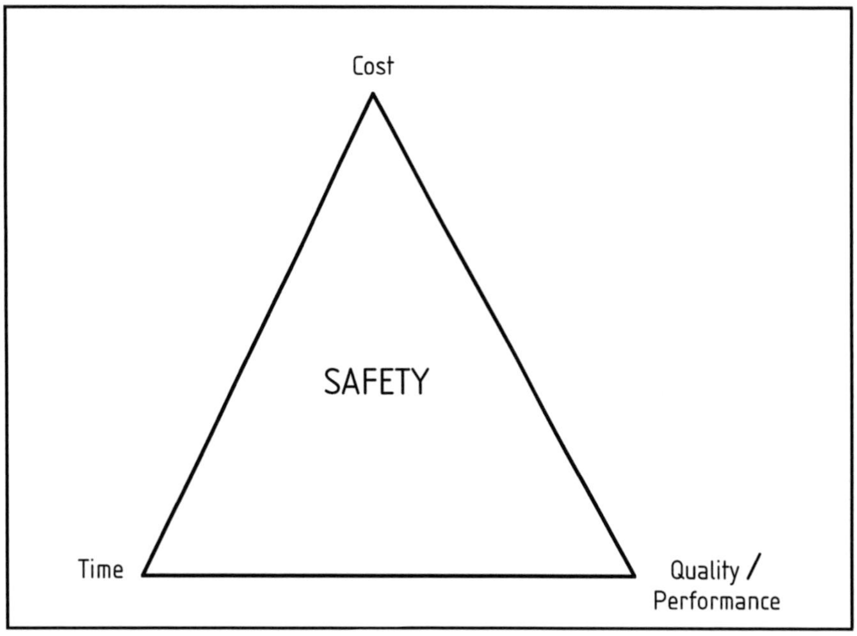

4.2.2   Custom and practice

Management in construction is influenced greatly by custom and practice. This can hinder the proper application of a project management system. It is common practice to simply adopt the management, or team, structure from the previous project, and not to question the roles and responsibilities of the project participants. It is equally common for a form of contract to be selected at an early stage, and for this to drive the organization structure, roles and responsibilities and even communication systems – whereas the selection of the form of contract should follow on from decisions about scope/project objectives, risk allocation and procurement strategy.

If the particular circumstances and objectives of a project are taken into account then this might lead to alternative arrangements to those customarily selected being identified as being more appropriate. Adoption of these alternative arrangements could significantly improve the outcome of the project.

In recent years custom and practice has been challenged by numerous initiatives aimed at improving the reputation of the industry and its delivery of projects. Custom and practice should always be challenged and should not be allowed to become a constraint on doing things in a better way.

4.2.3 The project environment

Construction projects, perhaps more so than projects in any other industry, take place in the wider geographic, social, political and regulatory environment. Whilst the immediate focus will always be on the client's requirements and the product delivery process – that of design and construction – wider considerations cannot be ignored.

Increasingly, the requirements of project stakeholders (neighbours, local residents, pressure groups and other third parties with interest in the project) need to be considered alongside those of the client when setting the brief for the project and the design specification for the product.

Design and implementation should take account of the social, political and environmental context in which the project is conceived and developed. Figure 3 shows the interaction between the immediate and wider project environments.

Figure 3   **Interaction between the immediate and wider project environments**

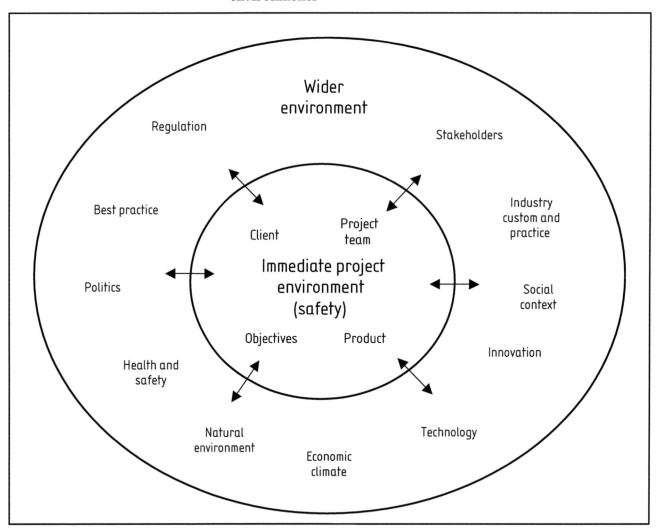

4.3 Projects and project management

4.3.1 Construction projects

From the client's perspective, a construction project is usually a part (albeit usually a large part) of some greater scheme. For example, a property development project is ultimately a project about adding value to a piece of land; the creation of a building is a stage in that process. Similarly, a power station development comes about to satisfy a need for electricity, and a factory development is part of a project to increase production capacity, or to make production more efficient. From the project manager's perspective, it is vital to appreciate, and always consider the relevance of the project in the client's wider scheme of things.

The client defines the scope of the project and the project team carry out the project on the client's behalf to produce the product – a building, or piece of infrastructure, for example. The client's project manager is responsible for managing the client's project. A project management system and project management processes should be designed and applied to the client's project by the client's project manager to ensure that it is successful.

The scope-related processes (Clause **6**) introduce the idea of a work breakdown structure in which the client's project is broken down into a series of tasks and sub-tasks. At the higher levels within this work breakdown structure, each of the tasks is a project in its own right – albeit a subproject of the client's overall project. Thus a feasibility study is a project, the design is a project, and the construction work is a project. Go to a lower level in the work breakdown structure, and construction of a building's frame is also a project, as is installation of the mechanical plant. There are usually many subprojects to carry out in a typical construction project. These form part of a combination of work elements that when completed produces the product and provides the client with the required benefits.

The principles of project management, and the associated processes set out in this Published Document, should be applied to the management of both the entire project, large or small, as the client sees it, and the subprojects. In every case, if a subproject is looked at analytically, there will be a client for the work, a scope will need to be defined, resources have to be applied, scope, time and cost control processes need to be applied and a product will be created at the end. In the case of a subproject the client might be a main contractor, and the product might simply be a component.

Figure 4 shows how a project, particularly one that might be multi-disciplined, can have several subprojects.

Figure 4   **Projects and subprojects**

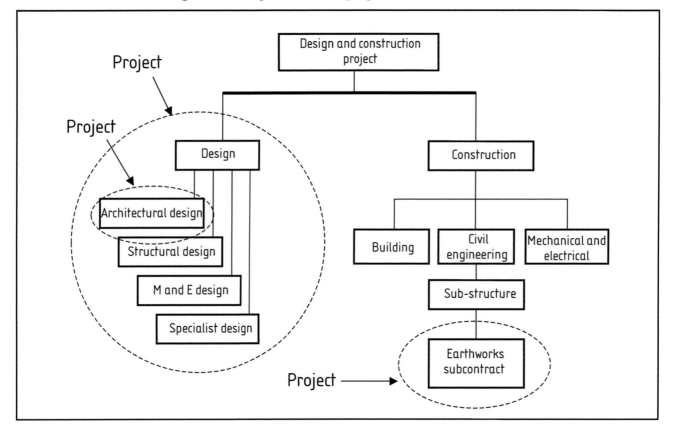

4.3.2   The role of the project manager

In the construction industry the term "project manager" is applied to an individual or organization that carries out a project management function.

The role of the project manager is sometimes seen to belong exclusively to the client's project manager, responsible at a high level for managing the entire project on behalf of the client. However, others equally perform a project manager's role in relation to the subprojects such as design or construction, or the management of a work package.

In the construction industry many different people perform project management functions, either wholly or in part, and at different levels in the project organization or at different stages of a project lifecycle. They are not necessarily labelled as project managers and might be termed contracts managers, agents, design managers, package managers, etc.

The processes and techniques set out in this Published Document are equally applicable to a small subproject as they are to the client's overall project. They are applicable to the client's project manager and to those people who do not necessarily have the title or label of project manager, but perform important management functions in the construction process.

4.3.3 Attributes of the project manager

A project manager needs to have enthusiasm, vision, dedication and integrity and should be able to generate these same qualities in the project team. The role requires technical but also interpersonal, communication, leadership and organizational skills.

In construction, a project manager requires a good understanding of the business, the organization and the processes used by clients, consultants, suppliers, contractors and subcontractors. Project managers also need to appreciate their own skills and limitations and those of their team.

The desirable attributes and skills of a project manager include:

a) leadership;

b) technological understanding;

c) evaluation and decision-making skills;

d) people management skills;

e) systems design and maintenance skills;

f) planning and control skills;

g) financial awareness;

h) buying and general procurement skills;

i) communication skills;

j) negotiation skills;

k) contractual skills;

l) legal awareness;

m) character;

n) project team building skills;

o) relevant experience;

p) social and environmental awareness.

These qualities and skills alone do not assure success. Success is only likely if the qualities and skills are applied with enthusiasm within a structured project management system made up of properly designed processes.

5 The project management plan (PMP)

5.1 General

The project management plan (PMP) is the document that brings together the project management system and the processes designed, and to be used, to deliver the project.

Its preparation is a fundamental prerequisite to properly managing a project, as it is the conclusion of, and physical evidence of, the necessary planning having been carried out. Its preparation is the responsibility of the project manager. The client and project team should assist in its preparation.

It should be an integrated management plan (see Figure 5) that brings together in one place good practice and the provisions of appropriate standards including:

- BS 6079-3 (management of business-related project risk);
- BS EN ISO 14001 (environment);
- BS 8800 and OHSAS 18001 (safety);
- BS ISO 10006 (quality management).

The PMP is an evolving document that integrates the principles, components and requirements together to achieve the objectives of the project. The initial PMP should be reviewed, refined and developed as the project progresses, usually at key control points through the project lifecycle (see Figure 6).

Adequate time should be allocated to develop the initial management system and to prepare the initial PMP and people resources.

Figure 5   **Integrated management plan**

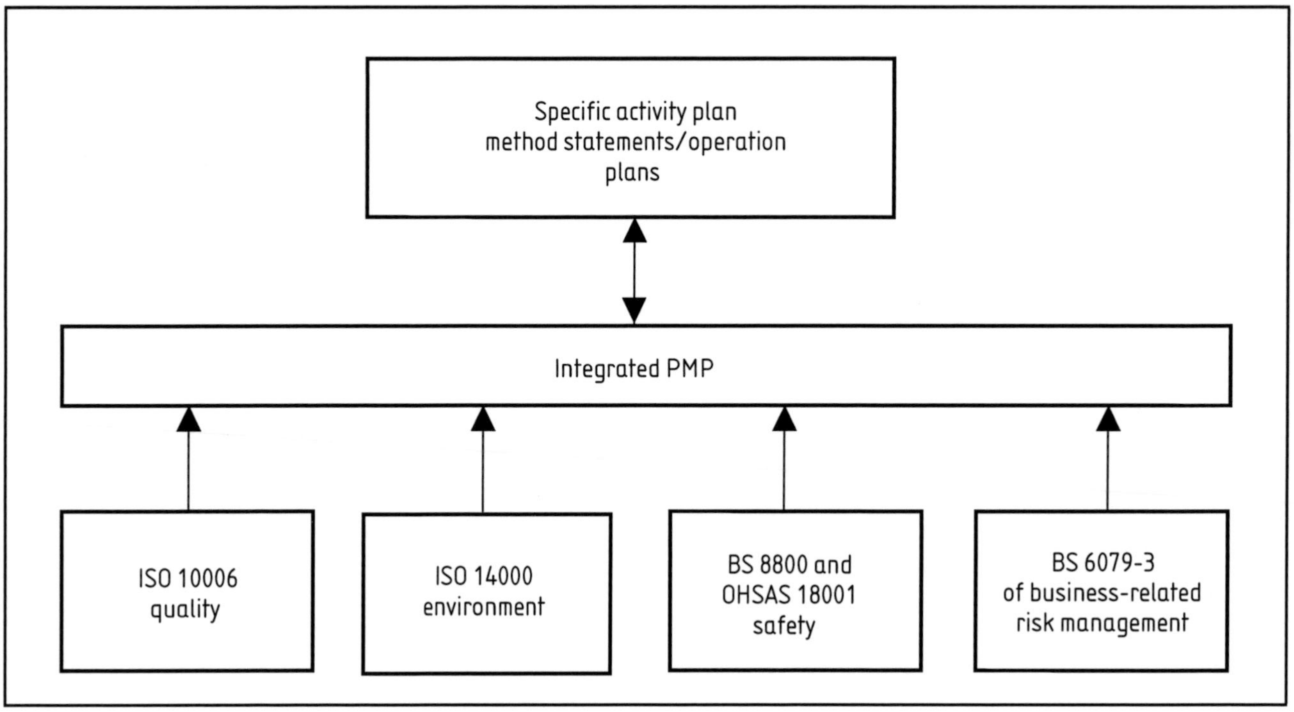

5.2   Quality management in projects

Projects should be managed in accordance with the principles of quality management (see BS ISO 10006). The quality management plan should be an integral part of the PMP. A quality plan should identify and detail the steps needed to produce the project deliverables, with the appropriate quantitative acceptance criteria, and the PMP should be designed to conform to the quality plan.

Figure 6   **Project lifecycle and control points**

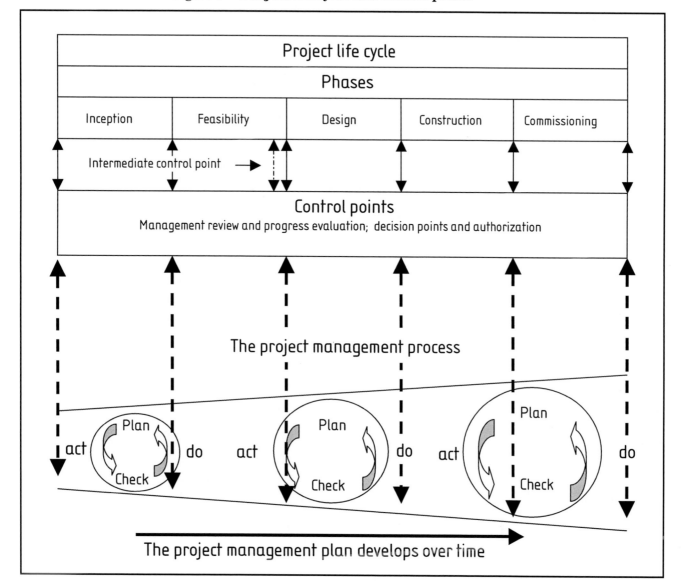

5.3 The components of a project management system

A project management system comprises a hierarchy of principles, processes, methodologies, techniques and tools. Figure 7 shows the components of a project management system and the application of each component.

Figure 7   **The components of a project management system**

Components of a project management system	Levels of a project management system			
	General	Industry	Business	Individual
	General principles of project management	Industry interpretation (How do the general principles relate to the industry and its legal and regulatory requirements)	Business interpretation (Specific and detailed corporate system)	Individual's interpretation (Individual's interpretation and use of the business system)
Principles	⟶ (arrow spanning General → Individual)			
Processes	⟶ (arrow spanning General → Business)			
Methodology	⟶ (arrow spanning General → Business)			
Techniques	⟶ (arrow spanning General → Individual)			
Tools	⟶ (arrow spanning General → Individual)			

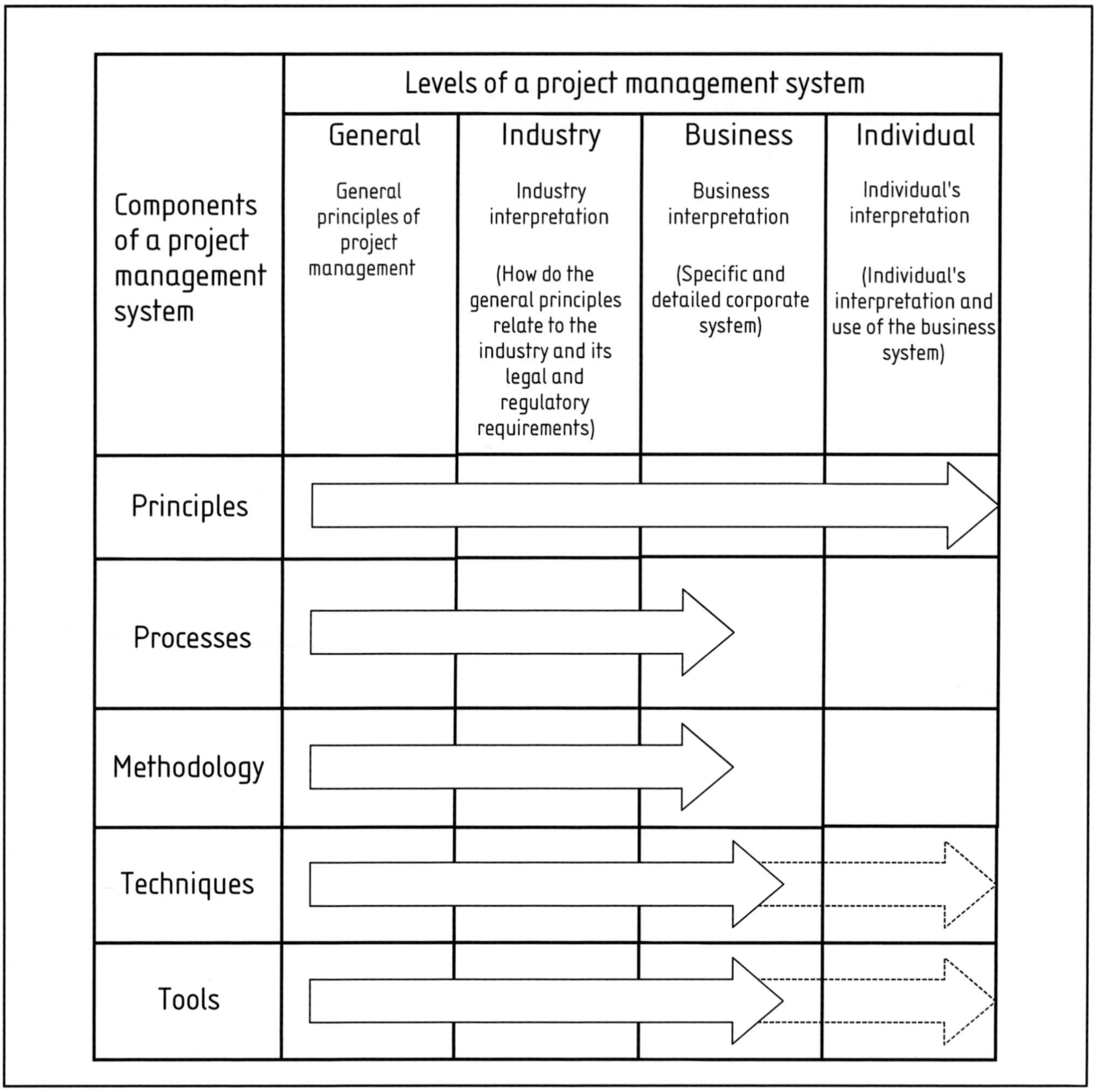

Figure 8 shows the variable and fixed project processes. It shows how the variable processes are adjusted to suit the requirements of each project.

Figure 8 **Variable and fixed project processes**

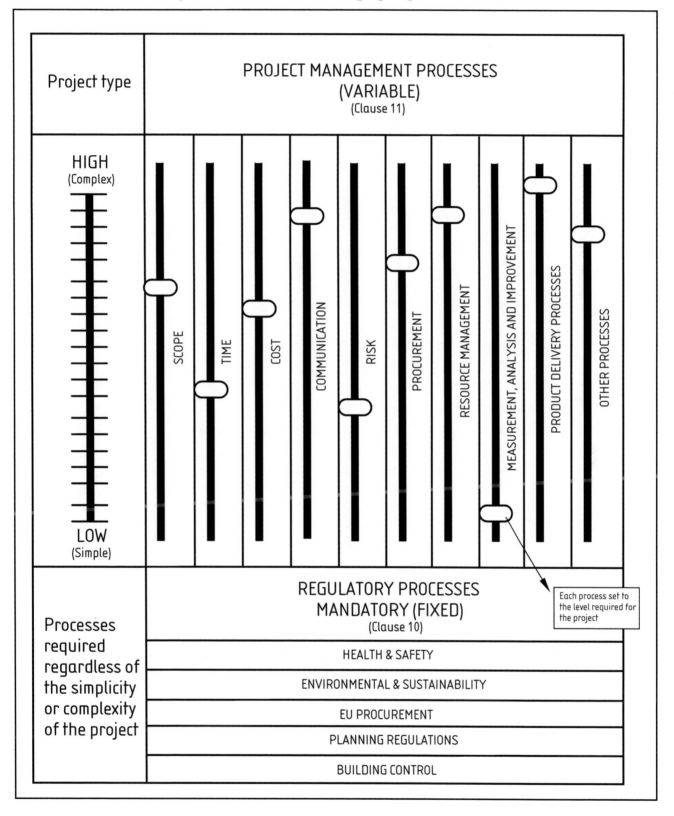

5.4   Project processes

A management process is a defined set of actions that convert a set of objectives into a product or set of deliverables. Resources are applied to carry out the actions. Figure 9 illustrates a management process diagrammatically.

Figure 9   **Management processes**

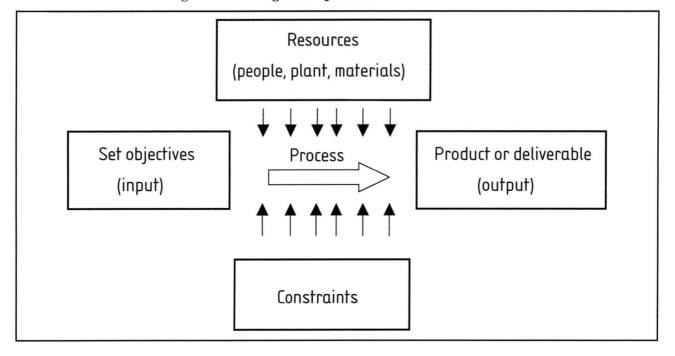

A linked and integrated set of processes can form a larger process, and eventually a system. Processes can usually be broken down into sub-processes.

Projects are controlled and delivered through a system comprising a number of integrated processes. Processes should be designed to achieve a particular purpose based on logic, experience and best practice. This Published Document identifies the processes that are, or might be, necessary to successfully manage a construction project. These processes are set out in Clauses **6**, **9**, **10**, and **11** as follows:

- Clause **6** (scope definition and scope-related processes): the process of establishing the scope of the project and then controlling the scope as the project moves forward;

- Clause **9** (product delivery process): the core process of designing, constructing and commissioning the product;

- Clause **10** (regulatory and enabling processes): the processes that run concurrently with the project delivery process with the aim of ensuring that the project complies with all appropriate regulations and best practice, and that enable it to proceed through, for example, the provision of necessary approvals and finance;

- Clause **11** (project management control processes): the basic project management processes used to plan activities, to set budgets for time and cost, to identify risks and apply resources, and to exercise control. These processes should be applied to any project or significant process.

Figure 10 shows the structure of a PMP and how the integrated processes come together in the document.

Figure 11 shows the way in which the regulatory and enabling processes are carried out concurrently with the project delivery process. It identifies with large arrows when the majority of the work is being carried out on any particular regulatory and enabling process.

This Published Document sets out best practice for all of the processes and sub-processes identified in Clauses **9**, **10** and **11**. The extent to which particular processes are applied will be dictated by the nature of the project in question. The project team should consider the application of every process and the degree to which it will be necessary to apply each one. Other processes might also be required as circumstances dictate. The project team should conclude whether additional processes are necessary and if so design them.

The project management control processes and the project delivery process can be as simple or complex as the project requires. Judgement needs to be exercised to define the extent to which they are applied.

Figure 10 **Project management plan**

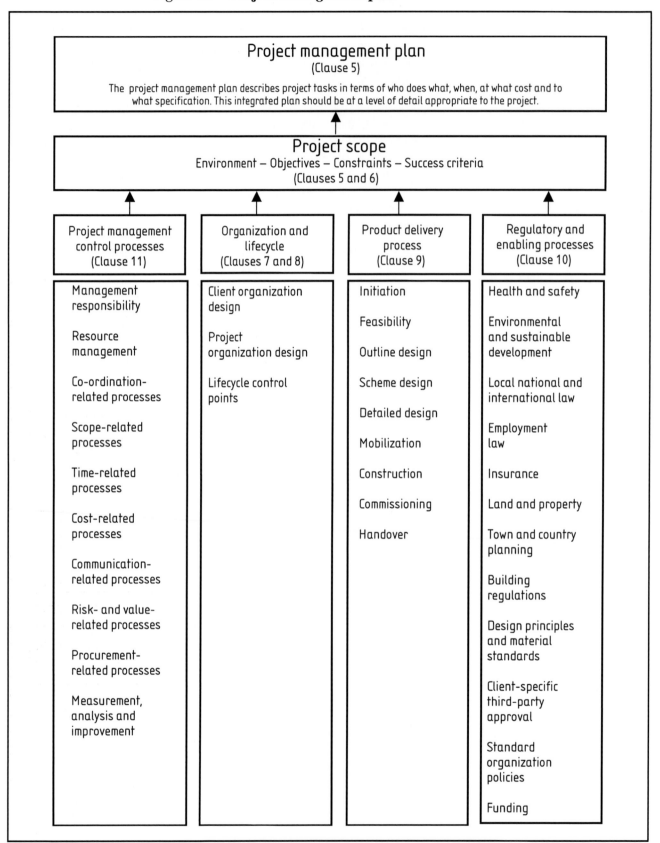

Figure 11   **The time relationship between the product delivery processes and regulatory and enabling processes**

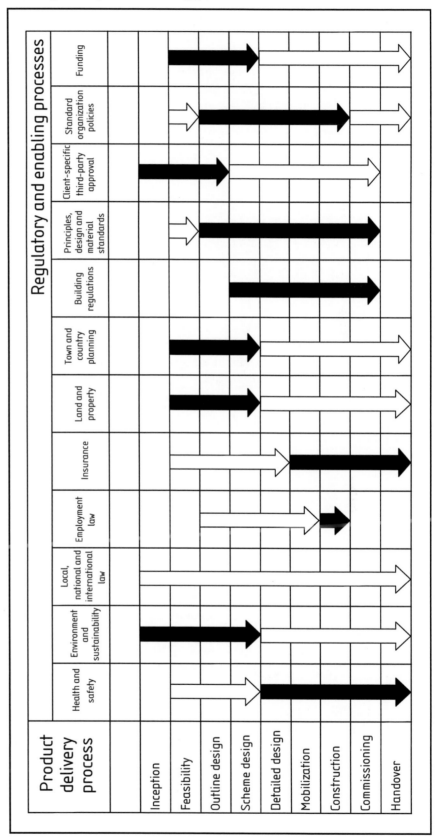

5.5 Hierarchy of plans

The PMP can generally be driven top-down as it is likely that the project will comprise a significant number of subprojects.

Each project participant should prepare a plan for their part of the project – their subproject. These individual project plans should then be integrated into an the overall project plan as indicated by Figure 12.

Figure 12 **Hierarchy of management plans**

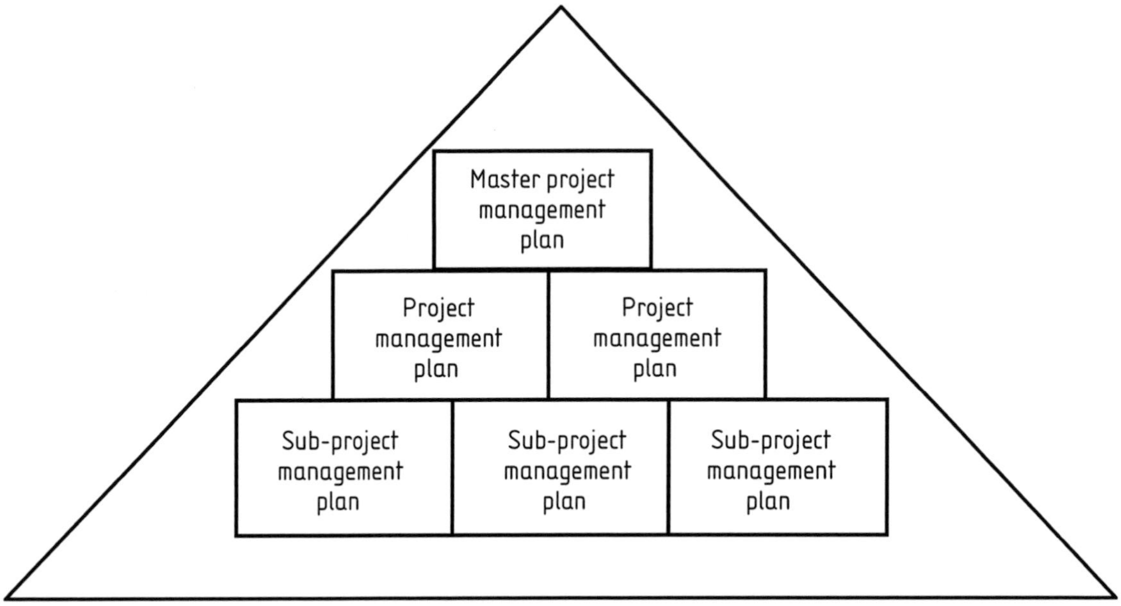

For the overall PMP to be effective, it is essential that it is communicated to the lower levels of the project hierarchy. The client's overall project manager should be responsible for preparing a plan for the entire project. Sections of the plan will need to be prepared by the other participants in the project, e.g. professional consultants, contractors, subcontractors, suppliers, etc.

The project manager responsible for each subproject should prepare each of the subproject plans. The detail of the sub-plans will be dependent on, and relevant to, the scope of the subproject. At the subproject level, for example, a designer is expected to produce a management plan outlining how the service will be delivered; a contractor is expected to outline how the construction process will be delivered and how the product will be delivered to the project objectives in terms of cost, time and quality in a safe manner which safeguards the environment. This may take the form of a generic management plan with an example of the specific or detailed management plan (often referred to as a method statement) that the contractor will produce for each activity or task.

Different levels of information should be requested at the different stages of a project's development. Table 2 shows the development of a typical contractor's project management plan from expression of interest through to handover. The same principle can be used for services and suppliers.

Table 2   **Development of a typical contractor's project management plan**

No.	Stage	Document	Activities
1	Expressions of interest	Not applicable	Letter confirming interest in tendering for a project
2	Pre-qualification	Information to prove that the contractor is a bona fide company with industry requirements in place for: • health and safety • quality • environment • financial stability • risk management • EU regulations • other relevant requirements	Declarations re: • health and safety • quality • environment Copies of certificates, confirmation that they have not been in breach of these requirements over a preceding period e.g. 5 years
3	Tender enquiry	• Submission of general project specific • Systems for health and safety, environment and quality • Schedule/programme information • Submission of activity specific method statements for early site activities or other key activities • Schedule of release dates for other activity specific work • Health and safety plan • Quality plan • Risk management plan	Opportunity to request a full project management plan rather than separate plans
4	Tender submission and assessment	• Assessment of tenders • Scoring matrix	Assessment of tender submitted
5	Contract award	Development of full PMP (see Table 3)	On contract award the PMP can be updated, reviewed, refined and developed Should include a schedule detailing key dates for the development of certain parts of the plan e.g. method statements, information release dates, design development, etc.
6	Construction/implementation phase	"Live" PMP	The PMP should be updated, reviewed and refined as necessary to meet the developing requirements of the project
7	Handover	PMP close out	The PMP should detail the requirements for closing out the project e.g. handover plans, commissioning and testing, as-built drawings, operating instructions and training plans for owner's own staff

Table 3 sets out the components of a typical PMP. The exact structure and details will be dependent upon the objectives and characteristics of the particular project.

The PMP is expected to develop during the lifecycle of the project. Due to the diversity of construction projects there might be variation in content, style and volume between one PMP and another.

Table 3   **Content of a typical project management plan**

Section number	Description	Contents and document control: distribution and amendment record
1	Introduction	Introduction to document
2	Project summary	• General description – project client, project name, project reference code
		• Project participants:
		• names, addresses, contact details
		• Summary of project aims and objectives
		• Business case
		• Summary of project scope:
		• schedule of work
		• statement of work
		• work breakdown structure
		• Project policies
		• Project approvals and financial and other authorization limits
		• Project security, privacy and confidentiality
		• Commitment acceptance, agreements, budget release and logs
		• Policies, standards, specifications, quality, health and safety, security and environmental issues
3	Scope definition	Refer to Clause **6**
		• Scope definition processes
		• Work breakdown schedule
		• Configuration management schedule
		• Change control processes
4	Project lifecycle	Refer to Clause **7**
		• Project phases – identify and clearly define project phases
		• Control points – identify and clearly define control points
		• Control points – actions at control points

Table 3   **Content of a typical project management plan** (*continued*)

Section number	Description	Contents and document control: distribution and amendment record

5	Project organization	Refer to Clause **8**
		
		Includes:
		
		• client/project interface
		• project organization:
		    • team organization:
		        • roles and responsibilities
		        • CVs of key people
		    • project staff directory
		    • terms of reference for project manager and staff
		    • directory of interested parties
		• function matrix
		• roles and responsibilities
		• management authority and delegation
		• communication
		• contractual relationships
		• resource management

6	Product delivery process	Refer to Clause **9** Includes processes for: • inception • feasibility • outline design • scheme design • detailed design • mobilization • construction • commissioning • handover
7	Regulatory processes	Refer to Clause **10** Includes processes for: • health and safety • environmental and sustainability • local, national and international law • employment law • insurance • land and property • town and country planning • Building Regulations 2000 [2], Building Standards (Scotland) Regulations 1990 [3] and Building Regulations (Northern Ireland) 2000 [4] • design principles and material standards • client-specific third party approval • standard organization policies • funding

Table 3 **Content of a typical project management plan** (*continued*)

Section number	Description	Contents and document control: distribution and amendment record

8	Project management processes	Refer to Clause **11**
		
		Includes detailed PM processes for:
		• management responsibility
		• resource management
		• time-related processes:
		  • project schedule:
		    • critical path analysis or network analysis
		    • milestones
		  • programme control
		• cost:
		  • cost modelling
		  • cost planning
		  • financial management and project account
		  • financial reports
		  • forecasts
		  • earned value analysis
		• communication:
		  • management reporting system
		  • data transfer methods and formats
		  • schedule of meetings
		  • project diaries
		• risk assessment and value management
		• procurement
		• subcontractor and supplier management
		• project and process closure
		• measurement, analysis and improvement
		• performance measurement, key performance indicators
		• dispute resolution

9	Appendices	
10	List of tables	
11	List of figures	
12	References	

6 Scope definition and scope-related processes

6.1 General

The first step in any construction project should be to define the scope of the project.

The scope-related processes:

a) establish a requirement for the project, and the benefits the client expects to obtain by undertaking it;

b) establish the client's brief, or set of requirements and constraints, for the project;

c) develop this brief into a scope and detailed specification;

d) break the overall scope down into packages for planning purposes; and

e) provide processes to allow change to be made to the scope in a controlled manner.

The processes aim to ensure that the final product secures for the client the anticipated benefits, that it meets the requirements of the client, and as appropriate that it meets the requirements of interested stakeholders.

Figure 13 shows diagrammatically the process of scope definition.

6.2 Inception – Client requirements and constraints

The client should initiate the project by identifying a requirement for a particular benefit, or set of benefits.

The client should establish an initial business case for any project, taking account of the whole life cost – usually having investigated other viable alternative ways to obtain the required benefit. The client should call upon the expertise of internal or external resources to establish the initial business case.

Having established that there is an apparent business case, the client should appoint a project sponsor to take charge of the project, from the client's point of view, and a project manager to manage the project.

The client should evaluate ways in which the concept can be progressed using internal and/or external resources, and an initial project team should be established to properly investigate the feasibility of the project.

The project team should confirm the requirements and the constraints that will be imposed by the client.

Client requirements typically relate to:

a) the benefits sought from the project, e.g. return on investment, payback period, etc.;

b) the functional requirements expected of the product; and

c) the timetable for delivery of the product.

Figure 13 **Scope definition**

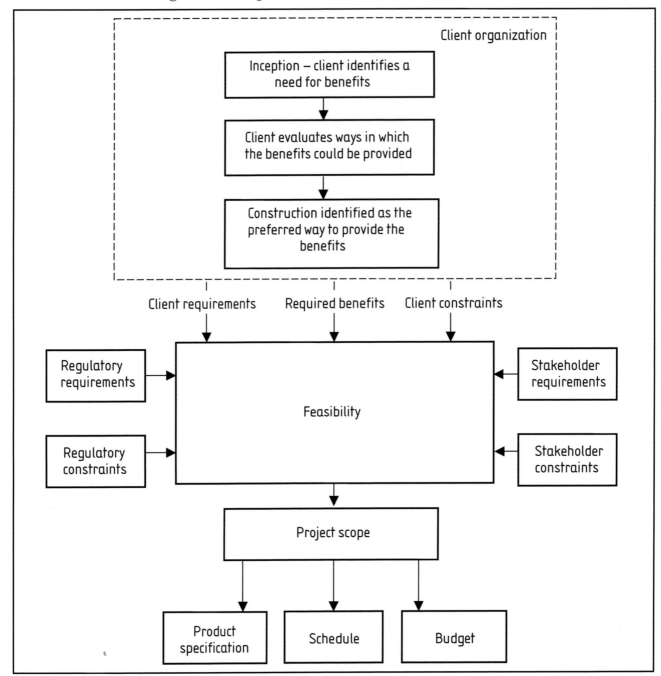

Client constraints typically relate to:

1) the available budget, and any constraints associated with cash flow;

2) the available resources; and

3) constraints imposed by the client organization, such as operating processes or when the site will be available.

There will be other requirements and constraints that will arise from the regulatory and enabling processes. The project team should establish precisely what these are.

Risk analysis and value management techniques should be used to fully draw out and explore the client's requirements, and the relative priorities to be assigned to them.

NOTE   *Guidance on risk management is given in BS 6079-3. Guidance on value management techniques is given in BS EN 12973.*

6.3 Stakeholder requirements and constraints

Stakeholder analysis should be carried out to identify:

a) all interested stakeholders (external and internal, positive or negative);

b) their concerns;

c) any legitimate requirements they might have relating to the project or product, and any constraints they might impose on the project or product; and

d) the influence they are likely to be able to exert.

The findings from the analysis should be recorded and, as appropriate, should inform the brief for the project, and the risk management plan.

6.4 Feasibility evaluation and the project brief

The project brief should be agreed and formally signed off by the client and the project team.

At the start of the feasibility phase, the project objectives are set by:

a) the client's requirements;

b) the client's constraints;

c) legitimate stakeholder requirements; and

d) constraints imposed by stakeholders.

The project team should identify and evaluate the options available to meet the project objectives, both stated and generally implied. The relative strengths and weaknesses of the options that are identified should be established and a recommendation should be made against the preferred option.

NOTE *Attention is also drawn to the regulatory and enabling processes (see Clause **10**) and the effect these will have on the product specification, the project budget and the project schedule for each option.*

Once feasibility is established, the brief for the project and the product should be formally documented. The brief should consist of requirements and constraints set by:

1) the client;

2) stakeholders; and

3) regulatory processes.

The project brief should form a clear and concise document from which the project manager can develop the project management plan, and from which the project team can work up the design for the product.

When alternative approaches and solutions are considered during the feasibility evaluation, these should be documented in the formal brief, with supporting evidence (including the analyses performed to evaluate between options, and other considerations used).

6.5 Scope development and control

The project brief initially sets the project scope.

The client should sign off the project scope at each control point.

The project scope should be developed and refined by the project team through the project lifecycle, particularly through the design phase. The project product's scope should be described through specifications, drawings, images, etc. Up-to-date characteristics of the product should be documented as completely as is possible, and communicated to the client and project team on a continuous basis. These characteristics should be used as the basis for future design and further scope development. They will also form the basis for other project management processes such as resource, time, cost and procurement-related processes (see Clause **11**). It is important that the input to the project management processes is, at all times, as current as possible.

The project management plan should include for regular reviews of the developing project scope to ensure that it continues to conform to the brief. Generally, the scope will develop through a process of adding further detail. Where the scope is changed, either through a request from the client, or as a result of opportunities or constraints becoming apparent through scope development, the change should be controlled through the change management process (see **6.8**).

The project team should consider how the product characteristics will be formally specified in tender documents, and how their conformity to requirements will be assessed during the construction phase. Drawings and specifications should be prepared accordingly.

The project scope should be fully set out in a formal report to the client prepared for each project control point (see Clause **8**). The project team should assist the client to fully digest the contents of any report and a presentation to the client of the project scope is often advisable to ensure that the scope is fully understood. Use should be made of techniques such as computer-generated images and "fly throughs" when appropriate.

The product and process characteristics should always be traceable to the documented requirements of the client and other interested stakeholders in the project brief for audit purposes.

6.6 Work breakdown structure

The project scope should be systematically broken down into discrete activities for scheduling, cost planning, work allocation, procurement and control purposes. The result is usually known as a work breakdown structure. The activities themselves are often referred to as tasks.

Activities, or tasks, should be broken down into sub-activities, or sub-tasks, to facilitate more detailed scheduling, cost planning, work allocation and control (see Figure 14 and Figure 15). The product and work breakdown structure is a way of developing and properly understanding the scope of the project.

Figure 14   **Example of a product breakdown structure**

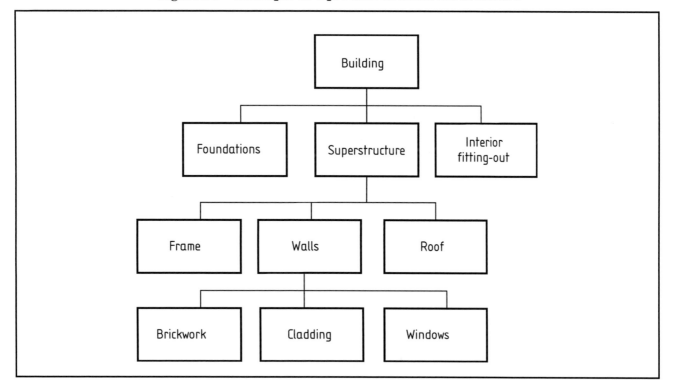

Figure 15   **Example of a work breakdown structure**

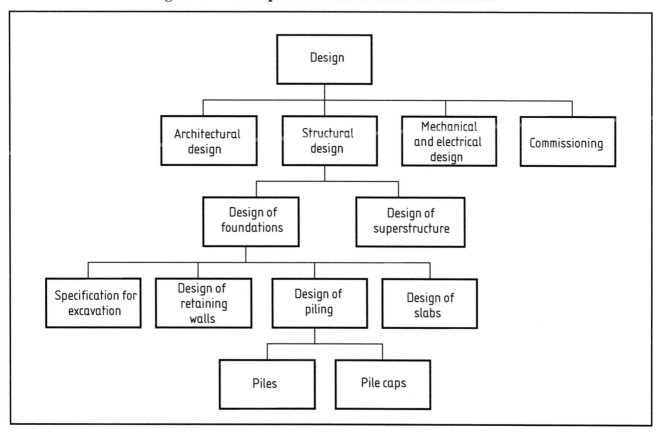

An activity, or a group of activities that are to be carried out by one organization, particularly where the organization is a works contractor, is often referred to as a work package.

To benefit from their combined experience, and to gain their understanding, acceptance and ownership, the project team should agree the scope of each activity.

The scope of each activity should be documented and should be signed off by the client, consultants and contractors as appropriate. Care should be taken to avoid duplication of scope across more than one activity, or leaving part of the project scope unallocated to an activity. Each activity should be defined in such a way that its results are measurable. The list of activities should be checked for completeness. The activities defined should include quality management practices, progress evaluations, and the preparation and maintenance of the project management plan. Responsibilities for each activity should be assigned.

The product may be broken down into component parts in a similar way to the breaking down of the project using a work breakdown structure. This time the breakdown is referred to as a product breakdown structure. A product breakdown structure is useful for cost estimating (**11.5**) and procurement (**11.8**).

6.7 Control of activities

The activities within the project should be carried out and controlled in accordance with processes documented in the project management plan. Activities should have resources allocated to them, a schedule, a budget, etc. Many activities will be interdependent. There should be close control of the interactions between activities to ensure full and proper integration and to minimize conflicts or misunderstandings.

Activities should be reviewed and evaluated to identify potential deficiencies and opportunities for improvement. The timing of reviews should be adapted to the complexity of the project, and the nature of the activity.

The results of reviews should be used for progress evaluations to assess process outputs and to plan for the remaining work. The revised plan for the remaining work should be documented.

6.8 Change management

Change management covers the identification, evaluation, authorization, documentation, implementation and control of change, or variations. It should be applied throughout the project lifecycle.

Before a change is authorized and implemented, the intent, extent and impact of the change should be evaluated. Thus its precise scope should be confirmed and any impact the change might have elsewhere on the scope, project schedule, or project budget should be evaluated.

Care should be taken to review the effect of the proposed change on the regulatory processes, and to take account of this. Consideration should be given to the contractual implications of introducing the proposed change. Those changes that affect the project brief, or the scope, schedule or cost last reported and signed off by the client should be formally agreed with the client and other interested parties before implementation. These changes can affect the contract value. However, where changes are required due to the contractor's internal modifications, it is usually expected that the contract value will not be affected.

Change management processes should be designed, agreed and documented in the project management plan. The change management processes should be written into the contracts between the organizations participating in the project. Change should be implemented in strict accordance with the mechanisms of any contract.

Change management processes should take into account:

a) managing changes to the project brief, project scope, and project management plan;

b) coordinating changes across interlinked project processes and resolving any conflicts;

c) procedures for documenting change;

d) continual improvement;

e) aspects of change affecting personnel;

f) operational factors; and

g) lifecycle maintenance.

If change is not properly administered, it can result in a negative impact on the project. Any such problem should be identified as soon as possible. Steps should be taken to resolve the matter as quickly as possible and should not be left until the end of the contract.

The root causes of negative impacts should be evaluated and the results used to produce prevention-based solutions and implement improvements in the project process.

6.9 Configuration management

Configuration management processes should ensure that the design and specification of the product is at all times properly updated as change is instructed or made, and that all parties who need to know about the change to the product configuration are advised of it.

The processes should ensure that there is a full audit trail to enable the source of particular change to be tracked.

NOTE   For further guidance on configuration management, see BS ISO 10007.

7 Project organization structure

7.1 General

Organization design is of critical importance for the successful outcome of projects. It is influenced by many factors, such as the project characteristics and the project environment.

A construction project involves bringing together a significant number of individuals and organizations to work together with the aim of translating the client's brief into the product. The roles and responsibilities of these individuals and organizations needs to be defined, together with how they will relate one to the other operationally and contractually. A number of organizational structures are regularly used in the construction industry; these are set out in Annex A.

Traditionally in construction projects, contracts have come first and roles and responsibilities have followed. A more appropriate starting point is a work breakdown structure (see **6.6**) that will identify the tasks to be carried out. Against this, roles and responsibilities should be identified. The nature of these roles will derive from the client's own capabilities, a general appreciation of the services and expertise available in the industry (architect's design and contractor's build, for example, and thus roles for a designer and builder can be defined), and the complexity of the project. For example, a novice client with a small project might elect to hand the whole project to a design and build organization, whereas an experienced client with capable in-house resources might choose the construction management route, engaging a full team of designers and a full team of works contractors.

Types of organization (e.g. architect, engineer, surveyor, contractor) need to be selected to take on the roles identified, and a structure needs to be drawn to link them. The nature of the organizations and the way they are linked together will be driven by a combination of the task to be undertaken and by client requirements, such as risk allocation. Only when the types of organization have been selected, and the structure has been drawn, should thought be given to the contractual arrangements that will formalize these links and give legal obligations to the organizations to carry out their functions. Only when the proposed contractual arrangements are set should the organizations that will fill the roles be selected using appropriate procurement processes (see **11.8**).

7.2 Internal client project organization

The client should determine how the project will interface with its core business activities and to what extent it wishes to be involved in the detailed management of the design and construction of the product.

The project organization structure should be established in accordance with the requirements and policies of the client organization and the conditions particular to the project. Previous project experience should be referred to when available, for the selection of the most appropriate organizational structure.

Clients that regularly carry out construction projects are likely to have an in-house organization with roles and responsibilities for the promotion and management of construction projects.

Where a client undertakes a one-off construction project, or programme of construction work, an internal organization, often referred to as a project board, should be established for the purpose of overseeing the project. The size and extent of the internal organization will depend on the nature of the project or projects, and their importance to the client's business.

If the project is important to the business, the main Board or equivalent management team should take a direct interest. A member of the Board should be assigned responsibility for the project. Clear responsibility and authority should be given for authorizing:

a) scope;

b) scope change;

c) budget approval;

d) schedule approval;

e) entering into contracts; and

f) payment approval.

The client might choose to put in place an internal project team, an entirely external project team or a combination of the two. The organization structure selected will depend on the capabilities of the client organization, the degree to which it wants to employ in-house resources with construction expertise and the degree to which it is willing to rely on external management for the execution of its project (see Figure 16).

Certain tasks can generally only be performed by the client organization, and cannot be delegated. These include:

1) setting and agreeing the project brief;

2) signing off scope, budget and schedule at control points;

3) approving and entering into contract with suppliers; and

4) making payments.

BS 6079-1:2002, Clause **5** outlines the primary forms of organizational structure available to a client, and the way the project organization relates to the main company organization structure. These are the hierarchical functional organization and the matrix organization. Examples of these organizational structures are given in Figure 17, Figure 18 and Figure 19.

The diagrams show the three basic forms of organization and the interrelationship between the corporate and project organizations in each.

In Figure 17, all work is planned, directed and controlled by functional groups.

In Figure 18, the project manager has executive authority over a team drawn from the functional groups. The team members are assigned full time to the project.

In Figure 19, individuals are allocated from the functional groups to work on the project as part of the project team on either a full-time or a part-time basis. Authority over subordinates is shared between the functional and project managers.

Clients can set up the necessary in-house team by seconding individuals onto the project on either a full-time or a part-time basis. The individuals either leave their usual job for the duration of the project, then go back to it, or continue with a reduced role in the main business at the same time as taking on project responsibilities. Interim managers can also be used to provide the client with dedicated in-house expertise for the duration of the project.

Where staff are seconded onto the project, care needs to be taken to properly define roles and responsibilities, both on the project and as necessary back in the main business. Human resources issues such as training, remuneration, etc. for the individuals concerned will need to be considered and addressed.

Figure 16   **Interface between the client's internal organization and the project organization**

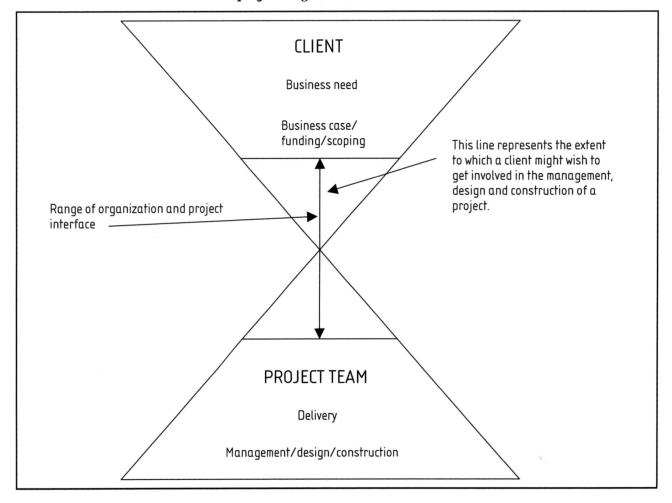

Figure 17   **Example of a hierarchical functional organization**

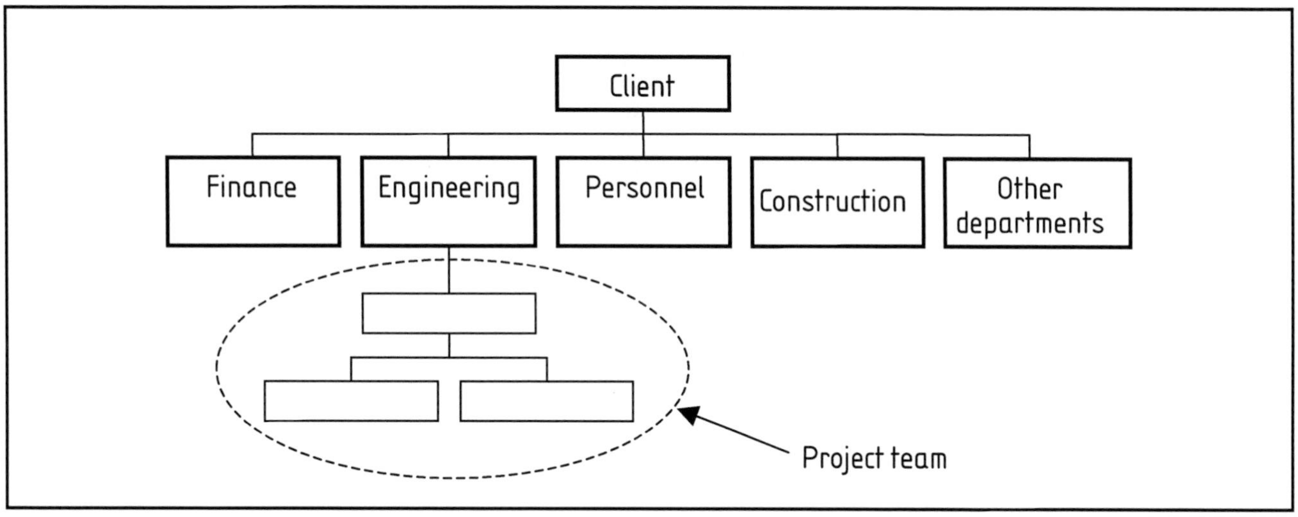

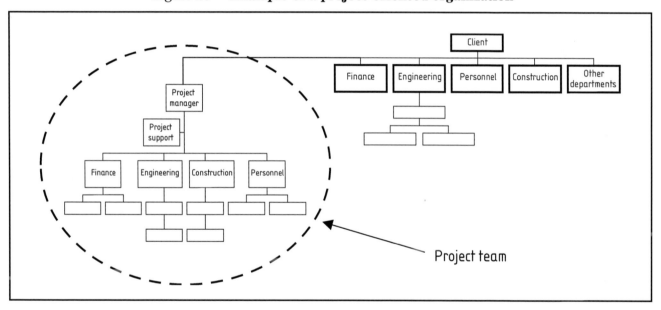

Figure 18   **Example of a project-oriented organization**

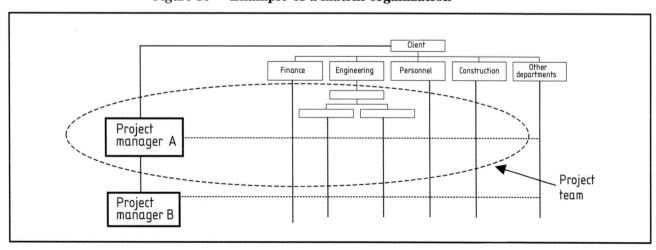

Figure 19   **Example of a matrix organization**

7.3 Project organization

A project manager should be appointed with overall responsibility for the project, and given an appropriate level of authority. The project manager should report to the project sponsor.

The project organization is responsible for delivery of the project. The project organization structure should be designed to:

a) put in place a team to carry out each and all of the functions necessary to deliver the project in an efficient manner;

b) make best use of the capabilities of available resources;

c) be appropriate to the project scope, the size of the project team, local conditions and the processes employed;

d) facilitate the desired allocation of risk;

e) relate to the level of management input the client proposes to make into the project;

f) ensure the necessary expertise is available to attend to each of the project processes, particularly the regulatory processes; and

g) facilitate effective and efficient communication and cooperation between all participants in the project.

The project organization structure should be documented.

The roles in the structure should be documented, together with related responsibilities.

The roles and responsibilities are a key input into the procurement plan (see **11.8**).

The roles should be filled using the procurement-related processes.

Interfaces with external stakeholders should be identified and documented.

The project function responsible for ensuring that the project's quality management system is established, implemented and maintained should be identified (see BS EN ISO 9004). The interfaces of this function with other project functions, the customer and other interested parties should be documented.

Reviews of the project organization structure should be planned and carried out periodically to determine whether it continues to be suitable and adequate.

7.4 Management authority

Management authority through the project organization structure should be defined. Roles and responsibilities should be clearly set down and documented. Reporting responsibilities should be defined, agreed and documented.

Responsibilities for decision making, financial and other approvals should be clearly defined, agreed, documented and communicated to all those that need to know.

7.5 Communication

Lines of communication and reporting within the project organization structure should be defined, agreed, documented and communicated.

Communication processes should be designed in accordance with the recommendations given in **11.6**.

7.6 Contractual relationships

Only when a project organization has been designed, and when management authority and communication lines have been set, should contractual relationships be considered.

Contractual relationships are necessary where an organization is engaged to provide a particular service to the client, or to another organization, as a means to fulfil a role within the overall project organization structure. The contractual arrangement should confirm and formalize the role and responsibilities the organization has taken on, the arrangements that have been agreed for management authority, arrangements that have been agreed in relation to communication and the commercial arrangements for remuneration of the organization for the role it is to play.

The outputs from the organization design process will form inputs into the procurement-related processes (**11.8**) in which an appropriate form of contract should be selected or designed to formalize the role defined during the organization design process.

7.7 Resource management

People probably have the greatest influence on organizational success. Care should be taken in recruiting, selecting, appraising and engaging the right people with the right skills. The resource-related processes (**11.3**) should be used.

8 The project lifecycle

8.1 General

The construction project lifecycle runs from inception through to completion – handover of the product to the occupier or operator.

Any project, irrespective of size and complexity, will naturally move through a series of phases during its lifecycle. In large projects the phases should be formally identified and separated to enable effective management of the project. For small projects the phases are usually less formal, but there can still be advantages in identifying them.

For management purposes the lifecycle should be broken down into phases. Typically these might be labelled inception, feasibility, design, construction, etc. Phases are important because the character of the work being carried out on the project will change from phase to phase. In consequence, the project organization structure (Clause **7**) could change from phase to phase too, as could the composition of the project team. Similarly, project processes could change from phase to phase. Processes are often confined to just one, or a number of phases, not to the whole project.

Identifying phases and subdividing them into stages is a useful way of breaking a complex project into clearly identifiable and manageable components. It also enables project management plans to be drawn, and processes and actions to be tied to a time line that is independent of calendar dates.

The end of one phase and the beginning of the next (through until the end of the construction phase) represents an increasing commitment on the part of the client. Each new phase requires a commitment to greater activity, more resources and greater expenditure. Each new phase also represents a closing down of the client's options – the scope becomes increasingly fixed, and making a change becomes increasingly costly. Each subsequent phase is also usually accompanied by a reduction in the overall level of risk. Figure 20 illustrates this diagrammatically. As a result, the boundaries between phases, or even stages, represent the preferred points in the lifecycle at which to carry out management reviews and progress evaluation (see **11.2**). They are also the points at which to set control points, decision points or gateways for obtaining approval and authorization before moving on.

Figure 20   **Changes in risk and commitment over the project lifecycle**

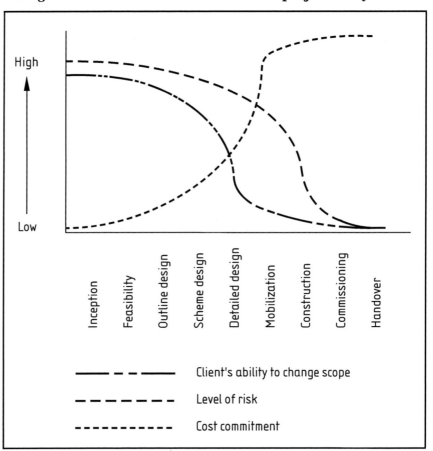

8.2 Project phases

The project should be broken down into phases, and then into stages that are relevant to the specific project circumstances. There are some standard lifecycles (or labels and definitions for phases) in use in the industry, but the labels given to the phases and the definition of the phases should be appropriate to the project. It can be helpful if the phases correspond to the product delivery processes (Clause **9**), and if the breakdown and terminology is familiar to the client and project team members. The use of one of the common lifecycles is therefore recommended.

BS 6079-1 identifies the generic project phases as:

a)   conception;

b)   feasibility;

c)   realization;

d)   operation (post-handover);

e)   termination (post-handover).

For a construction project greater definition is generally desirable.

NOTE   Annex B gives some of the more common project lifecycles, and phase names in regular use in the industry.

Some clients and some large contracting organizations have developed their own standard list of phases to suit their projects, processes and organization standards. This is consistent with good practice.

The phases and stages, together with the relevant work content of each, should be agreed and documented in the project management plan. They should be fully communicated to all, particularly stakeholders and suppliers, etc.

8.3 Control points

The client should provide formal authorization to proceed on to the next phase.

As a project proceeds through its lifecycle, the client's financial commitment and liabilities increase. At the same time its ability to influence the scope without time or cost implications for the project reduces.

As the project proceeds through its lifecycle the risk profile changes too. However, with greater certainty can come the realization that certain aspects of the specification might be difficult to achieve, that the anticipated schedule is too short, or that the initial budgets were too low.

The project lifecycle should contain a number of control points at which the project is critically reviewed to provide assurance that it can and should progress to the next phase. These control points are logically best located at the interfaces between phases as illustrated in Figure 6.

At each control point a full management review and progress evaluation (see **11.2.3**) should be carried out. Appropriate action should be taken based on the findings.

At each control point the project scope, schedule and budget should be reaffirmed to the client, designs should be presented for approval and the risk management plan should be updated and published. If the client is not satisfied with any aspect of the proposals to move to the next phase, the project team should revisit the particular proposal(s) until the client is satisfied and approval can be given.

The process of review and authorization at control points should be agreed with the client and documented in the project management plan. It should be appropriate to the scale and complexity of the project. Usually, the review process should be carried out internally by the project team, but external review can be beneficial where strict audit control will be applied.

Additional, intermediate control points can be inserted between project stages, or at predefined time intervals to suit project needs, if tighter control is necessary.

9 The product delivery process

9.1 General

The generic product delivery process in construction, which applies equally to subcontractors and to the client's overall project, is shown in Figure 21.

Whatever the size of project or subproject it should be managed using a number of integrated and complementary processes and sub-processes.

In parallel with the product delivery process run the regulatory and enabling processes (see Clause **10**).

The product delivery process delivers the product. The enabling processes allow the project to go ahead, ensuring that it is appropriately approved and that any necessary funding is available. The regulatory processes ensure that the product is delivered in a way that will comply with statute, the common law, best practice and any organization-specific controls relevant to the client, or its market sector. There will be links between the product delivery process and the regulatory and enabling processes.

The project management control processes (Clause **11**) should be applied to the project delivery process and each of the regulatory and enabling processes to provide management control.

An appropriate product delivery process should be designed and should be documented in the project management plan. The product delivery process should be integrated with and should run concurrently with the regulatory and enabling processes (Clause **10**). The project management and control processes (Clause **11**) should then be used to manage and control the project delivery process, and each of the sub-processes. Figure 22 shows the integration between the project processes.

Figure 21　**The product delivery process**

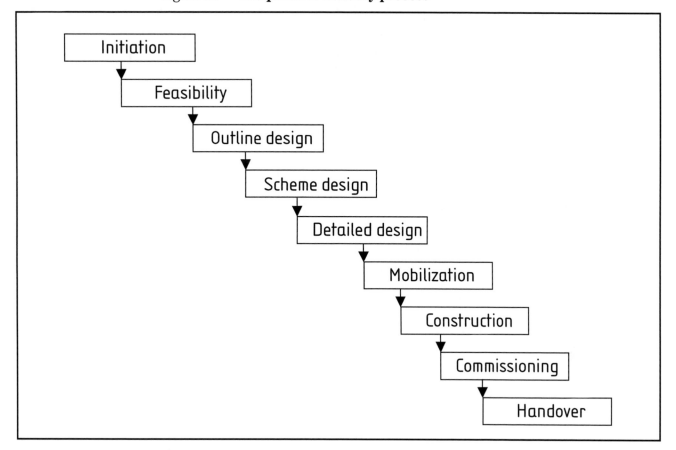

Figure 22　**Integration of construction project management processes**

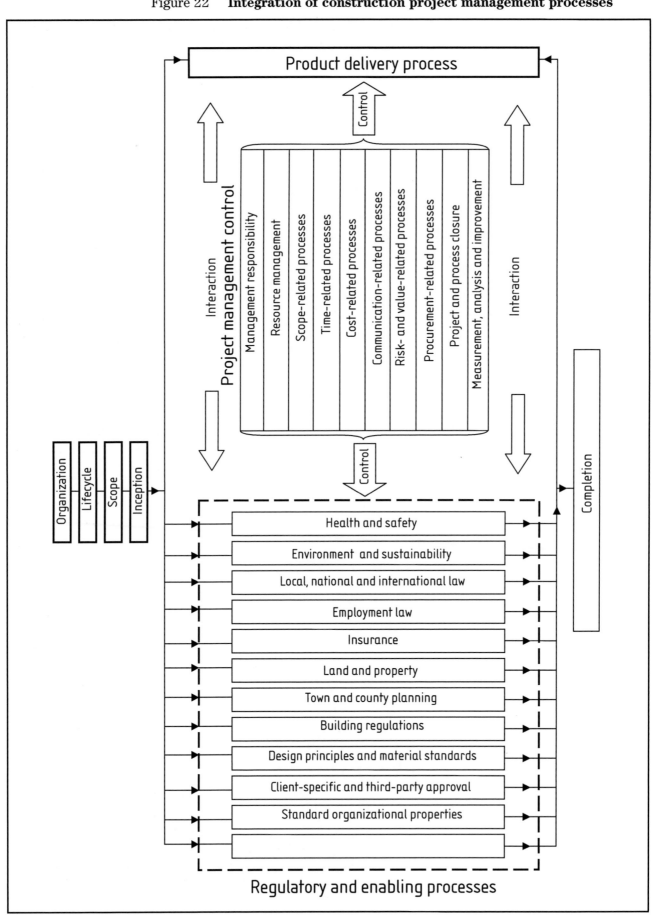

9.2   Initiation

The project is initiated when the client identifies a requirement that it believes can be met through construction work, and it initiates the project.

The client should establish an initial business case for a construction project, as described in **6.2**.

9.3   Feasibility

The feasibility process aims to confirm that the client's requirement can be met through a construction project, and to establish in principle the form of the product.

The project manager should identify in conjunction with the client those individuals and organizations that will form the team to evaluate the feasibility of the project. The project manager should procure the members of the team (see **11.8**) and brief them on the client's objectives. The brief should be documented.

The feasibility study should be thought of as a project in its own right and should be planned and managed accordingly. The deliverable, or product, should be confirmation that the client's objectives can be met, an outline scope, and cost and schedule projections regarding the overall project.

The project team for the feasibility study is likely to comprise as a minimum the project manager, a design consultant, a cost consultant and the client. It is beneficial to include representatives of the operator and appropriate specialists in the business of the client.

The feasibility process should clearly identify the client's overall objectives for the project, together with those of key stakeholders. These objectives should be documented. The process should establish other requirements and constraints that arise from the regulatory and enabling processes (see also Clause **6**).

The feasibility process should establish whether the client's requirements could be met in full given cost and schedule constraints, and the demands of stakeholders and the regulatory and enabling processes – or, instead, whether a balancing of competing objectives is necessary. As a result, the feasibility process might be iterative with objectives being traded off against cost and schedule savings to establish an appropriate balance to meet the client's requirements.

Feasibility should aim to conclude with a clearly defined written brief for the outline design stage of the project, and a control point.

9.4   Outline design

The outline design process should firm up a design concept, a preliminary schedule and a cost budget against the client brief developed during the feasibility stage. The output from the outline design process should allow an outline planning application to be submitted (if planning permission is necessary). The precise output required should be defined, agreed and documented at the start, and the process should end with a control point.

The project team should be reviewed at the start of the outline design. The team should be augmented by additional disciplines as necessary.

A lead designer should be identified in the discipline best suited to lead and coordinate the design (usually the architect in the case of a building project or civil engineer in the case of a civil engineering project). The lead designer should lead the design activity and report to the project manager.

A schedule, budget and functional cost for the outline design should be set.

The outline design process should be agreed in consultation with the lead designer, the project manager and the remainder of the project team. It should be documented in the project management plan. The project management control processes should be used to control the outline design process.

9.5 Scheme design

The scheme design process aims to develop the outline design to a level such that the scope can be fully confirmed and agreed. The product specification and design should be developed to a level to enable confirmation to be given that all of the client's requirements, including ease of build, can be met, or to set out precisely the best that can be achieved given the constraints operating. The form of the product should be clearly defined and suitably documented by the end of the process.

The intended output should be defined, agreed and documented at the start. The process should end with a control point.

Cost planning and scheduling should be taken to a stage that gives a very high confidence that cost and time projections will be achieved, such that firm budgets can be set for the project.

The output from the scheme design process should allow a detailed planning application to be submitted (where one is necessary) or otherwise secure preliminary endorsement from key stakeholders.

The project team should be reviewed at the start of the scheme design. The team should again be augmented by additional disciplines as necessary.

The lead designer should continue to lead the design.

A schedule, budget and functional cost for the scheme design should be set.

The scheme design process should be agreed in consultation with the lead designer, the project manager and the remainder of the project team. It should be integrated with the regulatory and enabling processes as these are likely to influence the design at this stage. It should be documented in the project management plan.

The project management control processes should be applied to the scheme design process to provide control.

9.6 Detailed design

The detailed design process takes the scheme design and works it up into detailed working drawings and specifications from which the product can be constructed. The output from the scheme design process should be full working drawings and specifications. The precise output from the detailed design process should be defined, agreed and documented at the start of the process. The process should end with a control point.

The lead designer should generally continue to lead the design. The exception to this would be if a specialist design manager is appointed where, for example, the design is being managed by a design and build contractor.

A schedule and budget for the detailed design should be set.

The design team should be reviewed and supplemented as necessary for the detailed design. Works contractors can provide valuable input and might be able to provide detailed design advice to the design team. Depending on project circumstances, it might be appropriate to appoint works contractors formally to the design team.

The detailed design process should be agreed in consultation with the lead designer, the project manager and the remainder of the project team. It should be integrated with the regulatory and enabling processes. It should be documented in the project management plan.

The detailed design process may run in part, concurrently, with the mobilization and construction processes. The detailed design of particular elements should be completed before those elements are constructed. The design of other elements scheduled for later in the construction process and yet to be constructed, may still be taking place.

Under some forms of procurement the contractor may undertake the detailed design process. Depending on particular arrangements, the make-up, structure and responsibilities of members of the design team may change. Where this occurs, responsibilities should be clearly defined and the revised structure, and corresponding responsibilities should be documented in the project management plan.

The project management control processes should be applied to the detailed design process to provide control.

9.7 Mobilization

The mobilization process involves the initial mobilization of resources – labour, plant and material – to carry out the construction work. In the case of complex, difficult, or overseas sites, mobilization involves arranging the logistics of getting the resources to the site, setting up the site and setting up all associated support infrastructure such as living accommodation, plant maintenance facilities, materials storage, batching plants, etc. It might be necessary to place a contract for advance or preparatory work, e.g. soil investigation or decontamination, before the main mobilization process can begin.

Mobilization is generally the responsibility of the contractor, but the client, client's project manager and consultants should be involved. Responsibilities for making the necessary arrangements should be set, and individual plans should be prepared. The plans should be integrated to ensure that resources arrive where they need to be, when they need to be there.

The project management control processes should be applied to each of the mobilization sub-processes.

9.8 Construction

The construction process involves the manufacture, fabrication and construction of the product based on the detailed design information. The output from the construction process is the product. The output from the construction process should be precisely defined in the building contract and in the output from detailed design.

The main contractor(s) should generally lead the construction process.

The main contractor(s) should procure resources for the construction, either in-house or through formal contracts with consultants, works contractors and suppliers.

The construction process should be developed by contractors if appropriate in consultation with the client, the project team and the client's other works contractors and suppliers, as appropriate. The management of construction process should be documented in the project management plan.

The project management processes should be applied to the construction process to provide control.

The construction process can be a complex matrix of sub-processes, and the methods selected should be integrated with the regulatory and enabling processes.

Where the detailed design process overlaps with the construction process, careful integration is necessary to ensure that design information is provided in sufficient time for procurement, further detailed design, fabrication and delivery to site to take place ahead of construction.

9.9 Commissioning

The commissioning process involves the commissioning, testing and approving of all the mechanical, electrical and control systems in the product.

The output from the commissioning process is the mechanical and electrical systems operating to specification and all necessary testing and approval documentation in place.

The specific deliverables from the commissioning process should be defined as an output from the detailed design process and should be set out in appropriate specifications and in the construction contract.

The commissioning process should be carefully scheduled and the schedule should be carefully integrated with the construction schedule. Adequate time should be allowed for the commissioning process. The time allowance should be reviewed regularly, and especially at control points.

The contractor should agree the detailed commissioning processes with those members of the project team responsible for specifying the commissioning requirements. As appropriate, the designers or a commissioning specialist should be engaged to oversee the commissioning process on behalf of the client.

The operator should be invited to be fully involved in the commissioning process to witness at first hand that the product has been properly commissioned.

The project management control processes should be applied to the commissioning process to provide control.

9.10 Handover and completion

The handover process involves the transfer of the product or facility from the project team to the operator. The output of the handover process is the product satisfactorily transferred to the operator, functioning as specified with all defects satisfactorily cleared.

The handover process should be fully discussed, agreed and documented between the project team, client and operator.

The handover process should cover the handover of all necessary operating and maintenance documentation and spares, spares schedules, maintenance schedules, etc.

NOTE   Attention is drawn to the legal requirement to provide a health and safety file.

Adequate opportunity should be provided for the operator to become familiar with the facility, and adequate training should be provided. The requirement for familiarization and training should be identified as part of the detailed design process and should be included, as necessary, in the construction contracts.

The handover process should allow for the joint inspection of the completed facility by appointed representatives of the operator and the project team. Any omissions or defects should be agreed and recorded. A schedule for rectifying any defects should be agreed and documented between the operator and the project team. Where a defect is the responsibility of a construction contractor, the contractor should be notified using the contract administration procedures set out in the construction contract, and the contractor is then responsible for remedying the defect in accordance with that contract.

The handover process should ensure that the operator puts in place all appropriate care and maintenance contracts. Checks should be made to ensure that the care and maintenance programmes put in place accord with the recommendations made by the installation contractors and suppliers to preserve the benefit of any warranties and guarantees.

Special attention should be paid to matters of insurance to ensure that there is no lapse of insurance as the facility transfers from contractor to operator, along with the insurable risks.

The project management control processes should be applied to the handover process to provide control, and should be closed out as full handover occurs.

10 Regulatory and enabling processes

10.1 General

Construction projects have a direct impact on the physical environment, and also on the wider economy, business, organizations, communities and individuals. As a result, there is a broad range of statutory regulation, common law, industry-specific control and published best practice that governs the way works can be designed, constructed and operated.

10.2 Design principles and materials standards

10.2.1 Published standards

Every country has professional bodies and trade associations which publish design codes and standards applicable to construction work. The guidance and recommendations contained in the codes and standards are not generally enforceable through legislation (although courts deem them highly persuasive), but they represent best practice and should be followed wherever possible.

The client and project manager should initially specify those standards that will apply to the project. The principal designers should specify those standards that will apply to the design and construction of the product.

The requirement to adhere to standards should be set out in formal appointments and contracts. Familiarity, or compliance with the required standards should be a requirement of the procurement process for a company, component or material.

NOTE   *Details of the different standards that are available are given in Annex C.*

10.2.2 Deleterious materials

A number of materials have become generally known either to be of hazard to health and safety, or to create long-term durability problems in buildings. These are generally referred to as deleterious materials. Building surveyors, property lawyers and large institutional investors, in particular, have become aware of these deleterious materials and will usually specifically exclude their use from any building they are advising upon, or are looking to obtain an interest in. Clients and designers should therefore ensure that materials known to be deleterious materials are not incorporated in the design and construction of buildings.

10.2.3 Sustainable materials

Many commonly specified construction materials come from non-renewable sources. These range from hardwoods to stone aggregates. Good practice, and increasingly legislation, means that designers need to specify materials from renewable sources, or recycled materials, for both temporary and permanent works.

10.3 Client and project-specific third-party approval

NOTE In many sectors the client's business is subject to special external regulation and the design and implementation of construction projects need to be referred to these bodies. It is the responsibility of the project manager to assemble a full and comprehensive list of all those bodies from whom approval needs to be obtained, and a full understanding of the nature of the approval necessary.

An approval plan should be prepared identifying each approval necessary, the party responsible for obtaining the approval, those involved in providing information, and key dates in the process. The approval schedule should be integrated with the main project schedule to ensure that the approvals processes do not delay the product delivery process.

10.4 Standard operating policies

10.4.1 Client operating policies

Many clients have internal operating procedures. Construction clients who regularly carry out construction work, in particular, generally have in-house processes and procedures with which they wish their projects to be managed. The project management plan should be prepared in full recognition of these policies.

Construction clients who have in-house processes and procedures, with which their projects are managed, should prepare those processes and procedures in line with the recommendations of this Published Document. The organization should prepare a generic project management plan. This plan should be adapted and amended to suit the circumstances of particular projects.

10.4.2 Project team member operating policies

Consultants, contractors and suppliers might have in-house processes and procedures appropriate to the management of the project. The project manager should take due account of any such procedures, and either use them directly or make use of them in designing processes and procedures for the project. There are advantages in using processes and procedures that the project participants are already familiar with.

Organizations are encouraged to design their in-house processes and procedures for managing projects in line with the recommendations of this Published Document.

10.5 Funding

Clients often need to obtain funding to carry out a construction project. The funding can comprise both short-term funding for the duration of the construction work, and longer term funding arrangements to fund the long term debt over the life of the facility.

The cost-related processes (**11.5**) should inform the funding process by identifying the overall budget for the project and the associated cash flow.

Specialist financial and legal advice is generally necessary to assist in securing appropriate finance.

The client is generally responsible for obtaining finance. It is usually necessary to provide information in the first instance to set up the finance agreement, and then to provide further information on a regular basis as the work proceeds. The project sponsor and client project manager should ensure that there is proper communication between the project team and those involved in securing finance, to ensure that the correct information is made available, and that responsibility for providing the information is clear.

The same management discipline should be applied to designing and controlling the funding process as any other process on the project.

10.6 Management of regulatory and enabling processes

10.6.1 General

Each area of relevant regulation and good practice, and each potential enabling process, needs to be considered when preparing the project management plan for a construction project. Specialist advice is often required to identify whether a matter is relevant and then to assess its impact. Not all potential areas will be relevant, but equally, and on occasion, further matters and issues will be identified through the process of risk management. In every case where an issue is identified:

a)   it should be properly identified;

b)   its effect on the project should be assessed;

c)   a plan should be formulated to deal with the matter;

d)   the plan should be implemented;

e)   implementation of the plan should be monitored to confirm that the planned objective is being achieved; and

f)   where there is a departure from plan, control action should be taken to address the departure from plan.

This sequence should be repeated at regular, pre-defined points throughout the project. The project management control processes (Clause **11**) should be applied as necessary to carry out these tasks. As the project proceeds, some issues might cease to be relevant whilst others that were previously of no concern, might become relevant – perhaps as a result of the design evolving in a difference direction, giving rise to a different impact on third parties. On each occasion the assessment, the plans for monitoring, and the control procedures need to be reviewed and amended as necessary.

10.6.2 Identification of issues

The identification of issues will often require the input of a specialist consultant such as a solicitor, planning consultant or specialist surveyor. The project manager should decide whether specialist input is required based on their own knowledge and expertise and that available within the project team.

When an issue is identified it should be assessed to establish precisely its impact, or potential impact, on the project and what will need to be done as a result. Specialist advice should again be called in as necessary.

10.6.3 Planning

Once the full impact of an issue has been assessed, a plan should be drawn up to deal with the matter. The plan should identify roles and responsibilities, key actions, timetable, cost and deliverables. The scale and detail of the plan should suit circumstances, and should be adequate to ensure the matter at hand is properly dealt with.

10.6.4 Monitoring

A process should be put in place to monitor activities to see that the plan is achieved. Usually this will entail seeing that pre-determined deliverables are produced to specification, on time and at the expected cost.

10.6.5 Control

Controls should be put in place to allow departures from plan to be addressed. The project management processes set out in Clause **11** should be considered in designing the controls. The extent of controls applied should be appropriate to the circumstances.

10.6.6 Review

On completion of the project the project manager and project team should review the regulatory and enabling processes that have been applied to identify improvements that can be carried forward on to future projects.

11 Project management control processes

11.1 General

The project management control processes should be applied to the project delivery process and each of the regulatory and enabling processes to ensure each has a successful outcome. The project management control processes are:

a) management responsibility;

b) resource management;

c) scope-related processes (see Clause **6**);

d) time-related processes;

e) cost-related processes including value management;

f) communication-related processes;

g) risk-related processes;

h) procurement-related processes;

i) project and process closure; and

j) measurement, analysis and improvement.

Figure 23 illustrates the project management control processes and how they are applied to the product delivery process and regulatory and enabling processes.

Figure 23 **The project management control process**

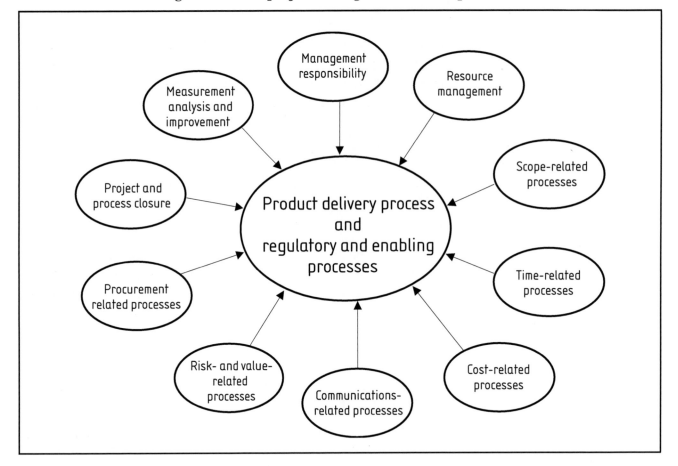

The following subclauses set out the project management control processes that should be employed to scope, plan, organize, monitor, control and report on the project, and to set the correct culture.

NOTE *Scope-related processes are described in Clause **6** and are not repeated in this clause.*

11.2 Management responsibility

11.2.1 Management commitment

The commitment and active involvement of the management of the client, consulting and contracting organizations involved in the project is essential for developing and maintaining an effective and efficient management system.

Management of each of these organizations should:

a) provide input into the design of project processes;

b) create a culture for safety, sustainability and quality;

c) actively create a culture that motivates the project team toward achieving the project objectives; and

d) provide a commitment to team development.

11.2.2 Project process

11.2.2.1 Process approach

A desired result is achieved more efficiently when activities and related resources are managed as a process [see BS EN ISO 9000:2005, **0.2**d)].

The project should be managed using a number of integrated processes and sub-processes. The project processes should be documented in the project management plan (see Clause **5**). Individual processes may be designed specifically for the project, or may be drawn from the client organization, from consultants or contractors. They should demonstrate good practice in the relevant area and may be a combination of processes from existing sources, drawing the best from pre-existing processes. The individual processes should be integrated. In selecting processes, the familiarity of the team with each process should be taken into account, as well as the efficiency of the process. The client organization should communicate the experience gained in developing and using its own processes, or those from its other projects, to the project team. The project team should take account of this experience when establishing the project's processes, but it might also need to establish processes that are unique to the project.

Processes should be kept as simple as possible to achieve the required result.

Process effectiveness and efficiency may be assessed through internal or external review.

NOTE   *The BS EN ISO 9000 family of standards provides guidance on a number of process-related and product-related quality management practices. These can assist a project team in developing appropriate processes.*

11.2.2.2 System approach to management

Identifying, understanding and managing inter-related processes as a system contributes to an organization's effectiveness and efficiency in achieving its objectives (see BS EN ISO 9000), and the project management system and organization should be designed with this in mind.

11.2.2.3 Application of quality management principles through the project process

Planning for the establishment, implementation and maintenance of a quality management system based on the application of quality management principles is a strategic, direction-setting process. In this planning, it is necessary to focus on the quality of both processes and the product to meet the project objectives.

11.2.2.4 Customer focus

Organizations depend for their future on their customers. They should understand current and future customer needs, should meet customer requirements and strive to exceed customer expectations (see BS EN ISO 9000).

Achievement of the client's requirements, and those of other identified stakeholders, is necessary for the success of the project. These requirements should be identified and clearly understood to ensure that all project processes focus on, and are capable of, meeting them.

The project objectives should include the product specification and its functional requirements. They should take into account the needs and expectations of:

- the customer – the direct project client, perhaps a developer (or a contractor in the case of a subcontract project);

- the eventual owner, occupier or operator of the product; and

- other interested stakeholders.

The project objectives should be documented in the project management plan and should detail what is to be accomplished (expressed in terms of product specification and quality, time for delivery, and cost budget).

The objectives should also set out what is to be measured. Measurement is necessary to allow proper monitoring to take place and hence controls to be applied to ensure that requirements are met.

The objectives may be refined or amended during the course of the project. When this occurs it should be through an appropriate change control process (see Clause **6**).

When it is necessary to determine the balance between time, cost or product quality, the potential impacts on the project's product should be evaluated, taking into consideration the client's and other stakeholders' requirements.

Appropriate lines of communication should be established in the form of a communication plan with all the interested parties to facilitate the exchange of information relating to the project requirements. Any conflicts between the requirements of the various interested parties should be resolved at the earliest opportunity.

Normally, when conflicts arise between the requirements of the client and other interested parties, the client's requirements will take precedence, except in the case of statutory or regulatory requirements. Throughout the project, attention will need to be paid to changes in the requirements of stakeholders, including additional requirements from new stakeholders that join the project after it has commenced.

11.2.2.5 Continual improvement

Continual improvement of the project team's overall performance should be a permanent objective of the project (see BS EN ISO 9001).

The cycle of continual improvements should be based on the Plan-Do-Check-Act (PDCA) concept (see BS EN ISO 9001).

Provision should be made, as appropriate, for self-assessments (see BS EN ISO 9004), internal audits and, where required, external audits (see BS EN ISO 9001) to identify opportunities to improve the project processes. Arrangement should take account of the time and resources needed, balanced against benefit to be gained.

11.2.2.6 Mutually beneficial supplier relationship

An organization and its suppliers are interdependent and a mutually beneficial relationship enhances the ability of both to create value (see BS EN ISO 9000).

The client and project team should work with its suppliers when defining its strategies for obtaining products and services. Contractors and works contractors should be involved early in the project if they can contribute beneficially to planning and design.

Risk sharing with suppliers should be considered. The benefits to be gained from a number of projects using a common supplier should be investigated where this is relevant (see BS EN ISO 9004).

11.2.3 Management reviews and progress evaluation

11.2.3.1 Management reviews

The project manager should review the project management plan, including its quality management system, at planned intervals, to ensure its continuing suitability, adequacy, effectiveness and efficiency (see BS EN ISO 9004).

11.2.3.2 Progress evaluation

Progress evaluations are regular reviews of project progress with a major review immediately ahead of control points between phases. The following specific recommendations should be met.

a) Progress evaluations should be used:

    1) to assess the adequacy of the project management plan and how the work performed conforms to it;

    2) to assess whether the project processes are running to plan, to identify any variances and the reasons for these variances, and to facilitate the planning of any necessary corrective action;

    3) to evaluate how well the project processes are synchronized and interlinked;

    4) to identify and evaluate activities and results that could adversely or favourably affect the achievement of the project objectives;

    5) to obtain inputs for planning the remaining work in the project;

    6) to facilitate communication; and

    7) to drive process improvement in the project, by identifying deviations and changes in risks.

b) Progress evaluations should be planned. The planning should include:

    1) the preparation of a schedule of regular progress evaluations (for inclusion in the project management plan);

    2) the assignment of responsibility for the management of individual progress evaluations;

    3) the specification of the purpose, assessment requirements, processes and outputs for each progress evaluation;

4) the assignment of personnel to participate in the evaluation (e.g. the individuals responsible for the project processes and other interested parties);

5) ensuring that appropriate personnel from the project processes being evaluated are available to provide information for the review or to answer questions; and

6) ensuring that relevant information is prepared and is available for the evaluation (e.g. the project management plan).

c) Those performing the evaluations should:

1) understand the purpose of the processes being evaluated, and their effect on the project quality management system;

2) examine relevant process inputs and outputs;

3) review the monitoring and measuring criteria being applied to the processes;

4) determine whether the processes are effective; and

5) look for potential improvements in process efficiencies.

d) Once a progress evaluation has been performed:

1) the outputs of the evaluation should be assessed against the project's objectives, to determine whether the performance of the project against the planned objectives is acceptable; and

2) responsibility should be assigned for actions resulting from the progress evaluation.

11.3 Resource management

11.3.1 Resource-related processes

11.3.1.1 General

Resources include labour, plant, equipment and materials and also facilities, finance, information, materials, computer software, services and space. Resource-related processes aim to plan and control resources.

There should be a clear responsibility and authority for the project's processes divided between the project team and other relevant interested parties (including the client organization). This division should be agreed and recorded.

11.3.1.2 Resource planning

All resources needed for the project should be identified. Resource plans should state what resources will be needed by the project, and when they will be required according to the project schedule. The plans should indicate how, and from where, resources will be obtained and allocated (see also **11.8**). The plans should be suitable for resource control.

Resource plans, including estimates, allocations and constraints, together with assumptions made, should be documented and included in the project management plan.

11.3.1.3 Resource control

Regular reviews should be performed to ensure that resources are available, and will continue to be available, to meet the project requirements. Deviations from the resource plans should be identified, analysed, acted upon and recorded.

Decisions on actions to be taken should only be made after considering the implications for other project processes and objectives. Changes that affect the project objectives should be agreed with the client and relevant stakeholders before implementation. Procedures should provide for changes in resource plans to be authorized by the manager responsible, as appropriate.

Revisions of forecasts of resource requirements should be coordinated with other project processes when developing the plans for the remaining work.

Root causes for shortages or excesses in resources should be identified, recorded and used as input for continual improvement.

11.3.2 Personnel-related processes

NOTE   Clause 7 deals in detail with the establishment of the project organization structure.

11.3.2.1 General

The quality and success of a project will depend on the participating personnel. The personnel-related processes aim to create an environment in which personnel can contribute effectively and efficiently to the project.

11.3.2.2 Leadership

A project manager should be appointed to the project as early as possible.

Leaders establish unity of purpose and direction for an organization, including a project organization. They should create and maintain the internal project environment such that people can become fully involved in achieving the organization's objectives (see BS EN ISO 9000).

11.3.2.3 Involvement of people

People at all levels are the essence of any organization, including a project organization. Obtaining their full involvement enables their abilities to be used for the organization's benefit (see BS EN ISO 9000).

Competent personnel should be assigned to the project. Appropriate tools, techniques and methods should be provided to the personnel to enable them to monitor and control the project processes.

In the case of multinational and multicultural projects, joint ventures, international projects, etc., the implications of cross-cultural management should be addressed.

Personnel in the project team should have well-defined responsibilities and authority for their participation in the project. The authority delegated to the project participants should correspond to their assigned responsibility.

11.3.2.4 Allocation of personnel

Management of the organizations comprising the project team should, together with the project manager, see that appropriate personnel are allocated to the project by the organizations.

11.4 Time-related processes

11.4.1 General

The time-related processes relate to project scheduling. They aim to determine the duration of activities and dependencies between activities, and thus allow the duration of the entire project to be established. The processes also relate to monitoring progress, assessing the impact of delay or prolongation, and to planning actions to ensure timely completion of the project.

11.4.2 Planning of activity dependencies

The project scope should be broken down into a work breakdown structure, and individual activities should be defined (see **6.6**). The interdependencies among the activities in the project should be identified, documented and reviewed for consistency.

Where interdependency involves a lag (i.e. there is a period of time that has to elapse before the follow on activity can take place), or where the follow-on activity can commence before the preceding activity is complete, this should be identified and the appropriate duration should be identified.

11.4.3 Estimation of durations

Duration estimates based on experience should be verified for accuracy and applicability to present project conditions. These estimates should be documented and traceable to their origins. When compiling duration estimates, the associated resource estimates should also be obtained for reference and as an input to resource planning. If the duration estimate is incompatible with the overall project time objectives, then a review of the network logic or ultimately resourcing might need to be carried out to meet the duration estimate.

Statistical techniques should be used as necessary to evaluate the magnitude of any contingency time allowance (see **11.7**).

11.4.4 Schedule development

Duration estimates from which the schedule will be developed should be compiled and checked for conformity to specific project conditions. An activity network (AOA or AON; see BS 6079-1) should be prepared linking the various activities on the basis of their dependencies. Activity durations should be applied to the network. The network should be used to prepare the project schedule, or schedules. Depending on the scale of the project, the number of tasks in the network and its complexity, the schedule should be prepared either manually or using a scheduling tool.

Whenever possible, during development of the project plan, standard or proven project network diagrams should be used to take advantage of experience. Their appropriateness to the project should be verified.

The relationships of duration estimates to activity dependencies should be checked for consistency. Any inconsistencies found should be resolved before schedules are finalized and issued.

The schedules should identify critical and near-critical activities, and a critical path.

The published schedule should identify events that require specific inputs or decisions, or ones at which major outputs are planned. These are sometimes referred to as key events or milestones. Control points and progress review points should be included in the schedule.

Standardized schedule formats, suitable for the different user needs, should be produced for particular uses or audiences. In the construction industry it is traditional to present schedules as a bar chart, although other formats are possible. The client and project manager will be interested in a high-level view of the overall schedule for the project, but a works contractor, for example, might only wish to see activities over the next month, but in far greater detail.

11.4.5 Schedule control

Progress against the project schedule should be reviewed regularly. The frequency of these reviews should be appropriate to the project and defined in the project management plan. Responsibility for reviewing progress and reporting should be defined in the project management plan.

Root causes for variances from schedule, both favourable and unfavourable, should be identified. Action should be taken to ensure that unfavourable variances do not affect project objectives. Causes of both favourable and unfavourable variances should be used to provide data as a basis for continual improvement.

Project progress should be analysed in order to identify trends that could cause possible departures from planned progress on future work.

Where progress departs significantly from the schedule, the schedule should be updated. This should be done to ensure that activities are again properly coordinated. Activity durations should be amended based on known rates of progress, or to reflect the impact of actions being taken to address the variance from the base line schedule. Dependencies should be adjusted as necessary.

The possible impacts of schedule changes on the budget and resources of the project, and on the quality of the product, should be determined after taking into account their implications for other project processes and objectives. Changes that affect the project objectives should be agreed with the client and relevant interested parties before implementation.

11.5 Cost-related processes

11.5.1 General

The cost-related processes aim to assist in the forecast and management of the project costs. This is intended to ensure as far as possible that the project is completed within budget constraints, and that accurate cost information can be provided to the client and project team throughout the project.

11.5.2 Cost estimating

Responsibility for cost estimating should be defined and documented in the project management plan.

When cost estimation involves significant uncertainties, or where the risk processes have identified specific risks which can have a cost effect, these uncertainties should be identified, evaluated, documented and acted upon. Allowance for remaining uncertainties, sometimes called contingencies, should be incorporated in the estimates. Appropriate techniques should be used as necessary to evaluate appropriate levels for contingencies. Wherever possible, contingencies should be specifically related to particular risks so that they can be managed. Lump sum contingencies to cover all eventualities should be avoided.

The cost estimate should be developed to provide a cash flow projection, identifying anticipated expenditure and income over time.

The cost estimates should be in a form that enables budgets to be established and developed in accordance with approved accounting procedures as well as project organization needs.

11.5.3 Budgeting

The client should formally agree and accept the budget and cash flow.

The budget should be consistent with the project objectives, the brief and the risk assessment. It should be broken down with allowances against specific project phases or activities, or both. Contingency allowances should be identified against particular risks and these should be documented. The budget should be accompanied by a project cash flow projection.

11.5.4 Cost management

Prior to any expenditure, responsibility for cost management should be defined and documented. The cost control system should be based on the work breakdown structure and be closely integrated with the procurement processes (see **11.8**). Cost should be monitored and controlled against particular activities or contracts.

The timing of cost reviews and the frequency of data collection, forecasts and reports should be established, agreed with the client and set out in the project management plan.

Root causes for variances to budget, both favourable and unfavourable, should be identified. Action should be taken to ensure that unfavourable variances do not affect project objectives. Causes of both favourable and unfavourable variances should be used to provide data as a basis for continual improvement.

At each review, the project organization should verify whether the remaining work can be carried out to completion within the remaining budget. Any deviation from the budget should be identified and, if exceeding defined limits, the variance should be analysed and appropriate action should be taken. As far as possible, particular activities should be managed such that costs are controlled within the particular work package budget. Any necessary expenditure of contingency should be carefully considered, approved and documented. Where it is not possible to contain over-expenditure within a particular work package, then confirmed under-expenditure against another activity should be used to fund the over-expenditure, avoiding having to increase the overall budget.

11.5.5 Earned value analysis

If it becomes apparent that increased costs will result in the approved budget being exceeded, the client should be notified immediately. An appropriate revision to the budget should be proposed, approved and authorized prior to further expenditure being incurred. Alternatively, an amendment to the product scope should be proposed, approved and authorized to contain costs within the budget. Revisions of the budget forecast should be coordinated with other project processes when developing the plan for remaining work.

The project cash flow should be regularly updated as the project progresses. The project organization should carry out regular reviews of the project costs, as defined in the project management plan, and take into account any other financial reviews (e.g. external reviews by relevant interested parties).

Cost management processes should be designed to provide the level of control and auditability required by internal and external auditors.

Project cost trends should be analysed. The plan for the remaining work should be reviewed on the basis of the conclusions from the analysis.

Earned value analysis can be used for monitoring and analysing costs, efficiency and progress, which are most clearly shown on the curves developed through the application of this technique. Those curves which are the end product of the analysis (see BS 6079-1:2002, **6.6.6** and BS 6079-1:2002, Figure 11) not only show the relationship between planned, actual and useful work done but can also be augmented by showing percentage complete and efficiency.

11.6 Communication-related processes

11.6.1 General

The communication-related processes aim to facilitate the exchange of information necessary for the proper management of the project. They ensure timely and appropriate generation, collection, dissemination, storage and ultimate disposition of project information.

NOTE   Further information is given in BS EN ISO 9004.

11.6.2 Communication planning

Appropriate communication processes should be established for the project, so that communication takes place regarding all necessary aspects of the project, including the effectiveness and efficiency of the project management plan and quality management system.

The format, language and structure of project documents and records should be planned to ensure compatibility. The communication plan should define the information management system (see **11.6.3**), identify who will send and receive information, and reference the relevant document control, record control and security procedures.

NOTE *For additional guidance on the control of documents and records, see BS EN ISO 9004.*

11.6.3 Information management

11.6.3.1 General

The project team should identify its information needs and should establish a documented information management system.

In order to manage the project's information, procedures defining the controls for information preparation, collection, identification, classification, updating, distribution, filing, storage, protection, retrieval, retention time and disposition should be established.

11.6.3.2 General communication and correspondence

The project team should ensure appropriate security of information, taking into account confidentiality, availability and integrity of information.

NOTE 1 *Guidance on information security management is given in BS 7799-3.*

NOTE 2 *Attention is drawn to the Freedom of Information Act 2000 [5].*

11.6.3.3 Drawings and specifications

The drawings and specifications that will be produced should be planned by the project team and scheduled. Planned dates for issue should be set out.

11.6.3.4 Contracts and agreements

All contracts and agreements should be formally documented, and original or authenticated copies should be safely retained by the parties.

Authenticated copies of contracts and agreements should be provided to the relevant contract administrator.

11.6.3.5 Meetings

Minutes of meetings should include details of attendance, the decisions made, the outstanding issues and the agreed actions (including due dates and the personnel assigned to carry them out). The minutes should be distributed to those present and relevant interested parties within an agreed time.

11.6.4 Communication control

The communication system should be planned and implemented. It should be controlled, monitored and reviewed to ensure that it continues to meet the needs of the project.

Particular attention should be given to interfaces between functions and organizations where misunderstandings and conflicts could occur.

11.7 Risk-related processes

11.7.1 General

The management of project risks deals with uncertainties throughout the project. This requires a structured approach that should be documented in a risk management plan. The risk-related processes aim to minimize the impact of potential negative events and to take full advantage of opportunities for improvement.

11.7.2 Risk identification

Risk identification should be performed at the initiation of the project, in advance of key decisions at project decision gateways and on other occasions when significant decisions are to be made.

The results from the risk identification exercise should be collated together with historical data from previous projects. The output of this process should be recorded in a risk management plan.

Risk identification should consider not only risks in cost, time and scope, but also, for example:

a) risk associated with the regulatory processes;

b) risks resulting from any proposed use of new technologies;

c) risks due to a failure of the project processes; and

d) risk associated with internal and external politics.

The interactions between different risks should be taken into account.

11.7.3 Risk assessment

Risk assessment is the process of analysing a risk and evaluating both its likelihood of occurring and its impact if it does occur.

Levels of risk acceptable for the project, and the means to determine when agreed-to levels of risk are exceeded, should be identified and documented in the risk management plan.

The results of all analysis and evaluations should be recorded and communicated to the relevant personnel and organizations.

11.7.4 Risk treatment

Solutions to eliminate, mitigate, transfer, share or accept risks, and plans to take advantage of opportunities, should preferably be based on known technologies or data from experience to avoid introducing further risk.

When a solution to an identified risk is proposed, it should be verified that there will be no undesirable effects or new risks introduced by its implementation. Any resulting residual risk should also be taken into account. The proposed action should be documented and communicated. Consciously accepted risks should be identified and the reasons for accepting them recorded.

Where contingency allowances are used to manage risk and are included in the time schedule or in the budget, they should be identified against the relevant risk headings and should be maintained and managed separately. All-embracing contingency allowances against risk should be avoided.

11.7.5 Risk control

Throughout the project, risks should be monitored and controlled by an iterative process of risk identification, risk assessment and risk treatment. An owner should be identified to be responsible for each risk requiring treatment.

Risk-related processes are explained in BS 6079-3.

11.8 Procurement-related processes

11.8.1 General

The procurement-related processes deal with obtaining resources, services and products for the project. These processes are relevant to all levels of procurement within the project. The purpose of the procurement is to procure resources to carry out the project, to procure components for the product, and to properly allocate risk.

11.8.2 Procurement planning

A procurement plan should be prepared in which the products (including services) to be obtained are identified and scheduled. The plan should take due consideration of the project brief, the proposed project organization structure and the product delivery process in identifying the products to be purchased. This plan is often referred to as the procurement strategy for the project.

The plan should identify:

- the products to be purchased;
- a specification for those products;
- method of procurement;
- the form of contract to be used;
- a list of proposed suppliers; and
- budgets and key dates in the procurement process.

All products and services that are used in the project should be subjected to similar controls, regardless of whether they are obtained from external suppliers or from the client organization (i.e. in-house).

To provide adequate procurement control, the project team should carry out regular reviews of procurement progress, which should be compared to the procurement plan. Action should be taken if needed. The results of the reviews should be input into progress evaluations.

11.8.3 Supplier identification, evaluation and shortlisting

Suppliers to the project should be evaluated. Evaluation criteria for suppliers of a particular product or service should be set in advance of the evaluation. An evaluation should take into account all the aspects of a supplier that could impact on the project, such as technical experience, production capability, delivery times, quality management system, safety policy/record and financial stability.

NOTE   *For further guidance on supplier evaluation, see BS EN ISO 9004.*

11.8.4 Documentation of purchasing requirements

Purchasing documents should be prepared for each product or service. These should set out:

a)   purchasing responsibility;

b)   procurement route (tender, negotiation, etc.);

c)   statutory procurement regulations (e.g. EU Procurement Directives [6]);

d)   associated legal or regulatory matters;

e)   bid evaluation procedure;

f)   procurement timetable;

g)   budget cost; and

h)   required delivery dates for the product.

The purchasing documents should also include documents describing the product or service to be purchased, and the contract conditions that will apply to the supply of the product or service. These documents will be used in either the tender or negotiation (the documents are commonly referred to as an invitation to tender). They should comprise:

1)   a description of the product's characteristics (schedule of services in the case of a design consultant, drawings and specifications in the case of a contractor);

2)   the timetable for delivery of the product;

3)   requirements to interface with other suppliers;

4)   appropriate quality management system requirements;

5)   insurance requirements;

6)   requirements for auditing (when necessary);

7)   right of access to supplier premises;

8)   the contract the supplier will be expected to enter into, including requirements for reporting, level of damages, etc.;

9)   any warranties the supplier will be expected to provide;

10) any requirements for bonds or guarantees;

11) the tendering documents themselves;

12) liquidated damages, where applicable;

13) dispute resolution procedures.

Tendering documents (e.g. requests for quotation) should be structured to facilitate comparable and complete responses from potential suppliers.

NOTE   *For further information, see BS EN ISO 9004.*

11.9 Project and process closure

Project closure is not completed until the customer formally accepts the project product (see also **9.10**).

At the closure of the project, there should be a formal handover of the project product to the operator. The process for handover should be planned. It should address all necessary demonstrations and training and ensure the handover of all necessary documentation.

The closure of processes and the project should be defined during the initiation stage of the project and be included in the project management plan.

Whatever the reason for project closure, a complete review of project performance should be undertaken. This should take into account all relevant records, including those from progress evaluations and inputs from interested stakeholders.

11.10 Measurement, analysis and improvement

11.10.1 Improvement-related processes

Measurement and analysis of data from the project should be produced to enable corrective action, preventive action and loss prevention methods (see BS EN ISO 9004:2000, **8.5**) to enable continual improvement in both current and future projects.

11.10.2 Measurement and analysis

Examples of measurement of performance include:

- the evaluation of individual activities and processes;
- auditing;
- evaluations of actual resources used, together with cost and time, compared to the original estimates;
- product evaluations;
- the evaluation of supplier performance;
- the degree to which of project objectives were achieved; and
- the satisfaction of customers and other interested parties.

NOTE   For further information, see BS EN ISO 9004.

The client organization's management should ensure that records of non-conformities and the disposition of the non-conformities, both in the completed product and the project processes, are analysed to assist learning and to provide data for improvement. The project team, in conjunction with the client, should decide which non-conformities should be recorded and which corrective actions controlled.

11.10.3 Continual improvement

The client organization and project team should ensure that the information management system for the project is designed to identify and collect relevant information from the projects, in order to improve the project management processes for other projects.

Information provided should be accurate and complete.

Annex A (informative) # Examples of project organization structures

NOTE   The following organization structure diagrams illustrate graphically the most commonly used organization arrangements in the construction industry.

A.1   Traditional management structure

Figure A.1 and Figure A.2 show typical lines of authority and contractual relationships in a traditional management structure.

Figure A.1   **Traditional management structures – Lines of authority**

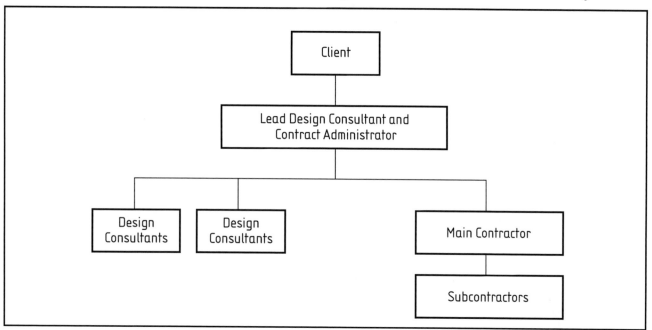

Figure A.2   **Traditional management structure – Contractual relationships**

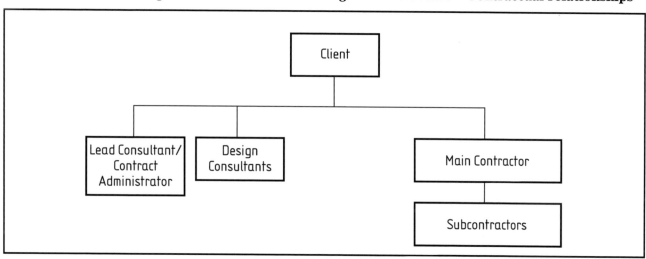

A.2 Design and build management structure

Figure A.3 and Figure A.4 show typical lines of authority and contractual relationships in a design and build management structure.

Figure A.3   **Design and build – Lines of authority**

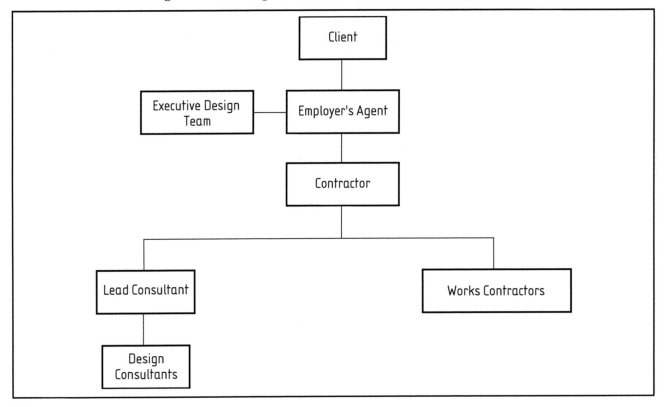

Figure A.4   **Design and build – Contractual relationships**

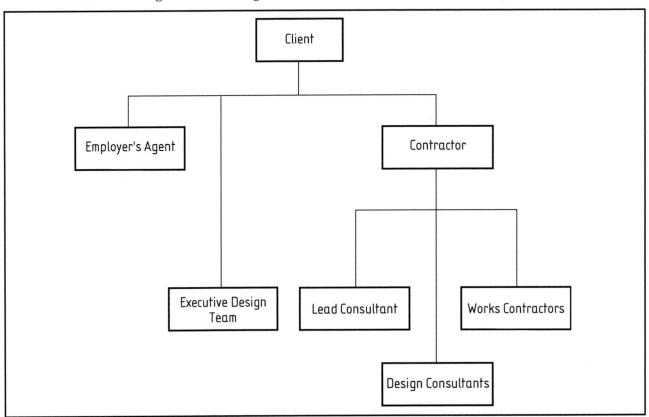

A.3 Management structure for construction management

Figure A.5 and Figure A.6 show typical lines of authority and contractual relationships in a management structure for construction management.

Figure A.5 **Construction management – Lines of authority**

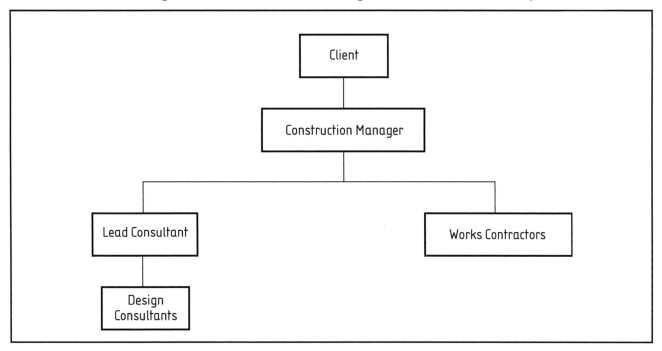

Figure A.6 **Construction management structure – Contractual relationships**

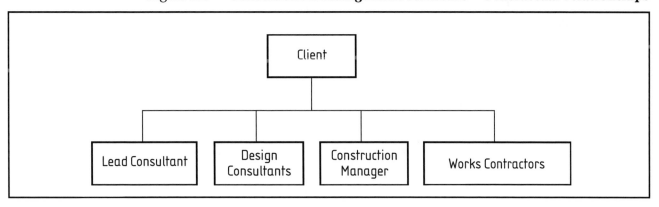

A.4 Turnkey management structure

Figure A.7 and Figure A.8 show typical lines of authority and contractual relationships in a turnkey management structure.

Figure A.7   **Turnkey management structure – Lines of authority**

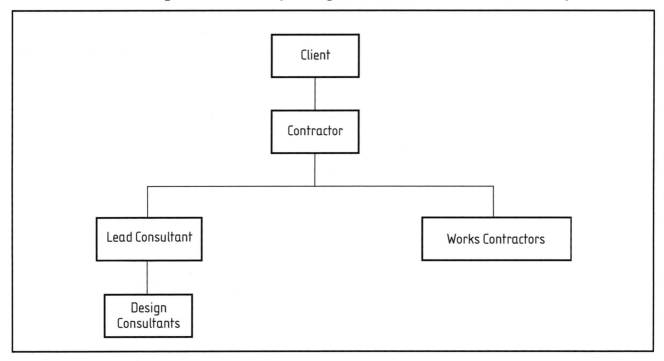

Figure A.8   **Turnkey management structure – Contractual relationships**

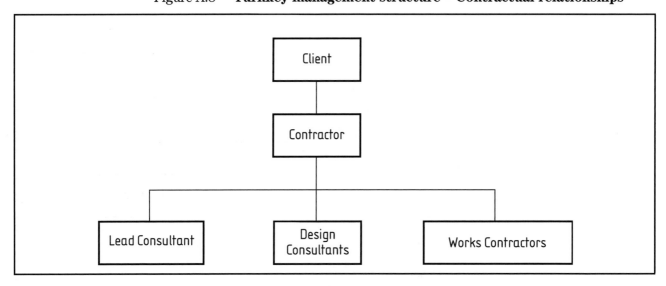

A.5 Management structure for executive project management

Figure A.9 and Figure A.10 show typical lines of authority and contractual relationships in a management structure for executive project management.

Figure A.9   **Executive project management – Lines of authority**

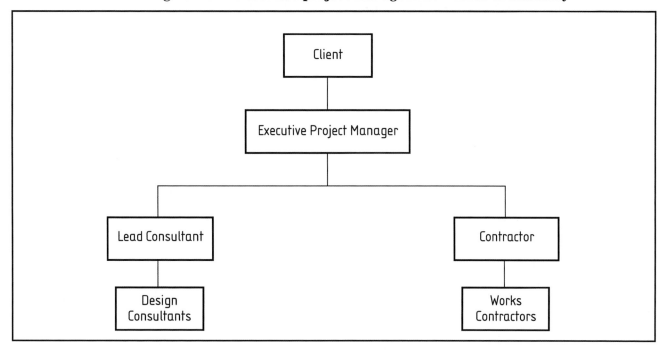

Figure A.10   **Executive project management – Contractual relationships**

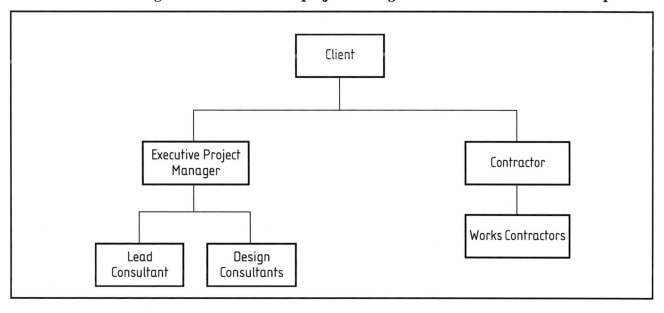

Annex B (informative)   Project lifecycles

Table B.1 illustrates some of the more common project lifecycles, and phase names in regular use in building projects.

Table B.1   **Examples of project phase descriptions used in the construction industry**

BS 6079-1:2002 project phases	Royal Institute of British Architects (RIBA) plan of work	British Property Federation (BPF) stages
1. Conception	A. Inception	Stage 1. Concept
2. Feasibility	B. Feasibility	
3. Realization	C. Concept	Stage 2. Preparation of the brief
	D. Scheme design	Stage 3. Design development
	E. Detail design	
	F. Production information	
	G. Bills of quantities	
	H. Tender action	Stage 4. Tender documentation and tendering
	J. Project planning	
	K. Operations on site	Stage 5. Construction
	L. Completion	
	M. Evaluation	
4. Operation	—	
5. Termination	—	

Annex C (informative)   Published standards

C.1   British Standards

The British Standards Institution publishes standards relating to management systems, design, products and materials. It sets standards of best practice for design and construction in the UK, which are used on projects overseas that are designed and constructed by UK practices and contractors.

C.2   ISO Standards

The International Standards Organization publishes standards relating to management systems, design, components and materials. It sets standards of best practice for design and construction across Europe, which are used on projects both in the UK and overseas.

C.3   Material and component standards

A number of trade and professional bodies produce standards for particular materials and components. They also certify materials and components. The standards generally represent best practice in the design, manufacture, installation or use of those materials and components. Certificated materials and components conform to these standards.

Bibliography

Standards publications

For dated references, only the edition cited applies. For undated references, the latest edition of the referenced document (including any amendments) applies.

BS 7799-3, *Information security management systems – Part 3: Guidelines for information security risk management*

BS EN 12973, *Value management*

BS EN ISO 9000:2005, *Quality management systems – Fundamentals and vocabulary*

BS EN ISO 9001, *Quality management systems – Requirements*

BS EN ISO 9004:2000, *Quality management systems – Guidelines for performance improvements*

BS ISO 10007, *Quality management systems – Guidelines for configuration management*

Other publications

[1] GREAT BRITAIN. Construction (Design and Management) Regulations 1994 and subsequent amendments. London: HMSO.

[2] GREAT BRITAIN. Building Regulations 2000 and subsequent amendments. London: The Stationery Office.

[3] GREAT BRITAIN. Building Standards (Scotland) Regulations 1990 and subsequent amendments. London: HMSO.

[4] GREAT BRITAIN. Building Regulations (Northern Ireland) 2000. London: The Stationery Office.

[5] GREAT BRITAIN. Freedom of Information Act 2000. London: The Stationery Office.

[6] EUROPEAN COMMUNITIES. 98/4/EC. EC Procurement Directives Directive 98/4/EC of the European Parliament and of the Council of 16 February 1998 amending Directive 93/38/EEC coordinating the procurement procedures of entities operating in the water, energy, transport and telecommunications sectors. Luxembourg: Office for Official Publications of the European Communities, 1998.

Further reading and information

BOURN, Sir John, on behalf of the NATIONAL AUDIT OFFICE. *Modernising construction – Report by the Comptroller and Auditor General, HC 87 Session 2000–2001 ("The Latham Report")*. London: The Stationery Office, 2001.
http://www.nao.org.uk/publications/nao_reports/00-01/000187.pdf

CHARTERED INSTITUTE OF BUILDING. *Code of practice for project management for construction and development*. Third edition. Oxford/Edinburgh: Blackwell Science, 2002. ISBN 1405103094.

CONSTRUCTION TASK FORCE TO THE DEPUTY PRIME MINISTER. *Rethinking Construction ("The Egan Report")*. London: Department of Trade and Industry Construction Sector Unit, 1998. http://www.dti.gov.uk/construction/rethink/report/

OFFICE OF GOVERNMENT COMMERCE. *Achieving excellence guides*. London: Office of Government Commerce, 2003–2005. http://www.ogc.gov.uk/sdtoolkit/reference/ogc_library/achievingexcellence/